Of all the problems facing the heritage industry today, the management of gardens and their landscape environment create some of the greatest difficulties. Many gardens have an artistic, historic or cultural significance above and beyond mere recreational enjoyment. It is all too easy to bury a garden's more transient features under fashionable, modern planting schemes, or to lose its original features completely in misguided attempts to simplify maintenance.

Heritage Gardens shows how to avoid such pitfalls, giving practical advice about garden design, management planning and maintenance. But it is more than just a practical handbook. It is a guide to all aspects of the conservation of gardens within the context of the history of the development of garden design in Europe and America, from the assessment of a garden's merit to the making of policy decisions. It examines the responsibilities of owners, and looks at the role of governments, national and international bodies in listing, legislation and grant aid. Case studies drawn from five different countries are used to illustrate different approaches and problems, and detailed sources of further information are provided.

The book will prove invaluable for professionals – landscape architects, planners, conservation officers and gardeners – and students specialising in conservation issues. It will also appeal to anyone interested in historic gardens and conservation issues in general.

Sheena **Mackellar Goulty** is a landscape architect specialising in the conservation of gardens and estate policies working in both Scotland and Italy.

THE HERITAGE
CARE
PRESERVATION
MANAGEMENT

Editor in chief Andrew Wheatcroft

The Heritage: Care–Preservation–Management programme has been designed to serve the needs of the museum and heritage community worldwide. It publishes books and information services for professional museum and heritage workers, and for all the organisations that service the museum community.

The programme has been devised with the advice and assistance of the leading institutions in the museum and heritage community, at an international level, with ICOM and ICOMOS, with the national and local museum organisations and with individual specialists drawn from every continent.

Forward Planning: *A handbook of business, corporate and development planning for museums and galleries*
Edited by Timothy Ambrose and Sue Runyard

The Industrial Heritage: *Managing resources and uses*
Judith Alfrey and Tim Putnam

Museum Basics
Timothy Ambrose and Crispin Paine

Museum Security and Protection: *A handbook for cultural heritage institutions*
ICOM and ICMS

Museums 2000: *Politics, people, professionals and profit*
Edited by Patrick J. Boylan

Museums and the Shaping of Knowledge
Eilean Hooper-Greenhill

Museums without Barriers: *A new deal for disabled people*
Fondation de France and ICOM

The Past in Contemporary Society: Then/Now
P. J. Fowler

The Representation of the Past: *Museums and heritage in the post-modern world*
Kevin Walsh

Heritage Gardens

Care, conservation and management

Sheena Mackellar Goulty

London and New York

First published 1993
by Routledge
11 New Fetter Lane, London EC4P 4EE

Simultaneously published in the USA and Canada
by Routledge Inc.
29 West 35th Street, New York, NY 10001

Filmset by Selwood Systems, Midsomer Norton
Printed and bound in Great Britain by
Butler & Tanner Ltd, Frome and London

(∞) printed on paper manufactured in
accordance with the proposed
ANSI/NISO Z 39.48–199X and
ANSI Z 39.48–1984

British Library Cataloguing in Publication Data

Goulty, Sheena Mackellar,
    Heritage gardens: care, conservation and management.
    I. Title
    712.6

Library of Congress Cataloging in Publication Data

Goulty, Sheena Mackellar,
    Heritage gardens: care, conservation and management/Sheena Mackellar Goulty.
        p.   cm.
    Includes bibliographical references.
    1. Historic gardens – Conservation and restoration. 2. Gardens –
    Conservation and restoration. 3. Historic gardens – Management.
    4. Gardens – Management. I. Title.
    SB467.G68   1992
    635.9–dc20   91–46366
        ISBN 0–415–07474–6

Other echoes inhabit the garden
T. S. Eliot

For
Iain Taylor Carruthers
1947–1986

Dimly, the shadows of my age
Haze on the memory of snowdrop mornings;
Blue lupins. And now the breath
That once was spring
Coughs to the chime of cacophonic bells.
I. T. Carruthers

Contents

Illustrations

Illustrations

Preface

Gardens where a soul's at ease;
Where everything that meets the eye,
Flowers and grass and cloudless sky,
Resemble forms that are or seem
When sleepers wake and yet still dream.
                                        W. B. Yeats

Gardens have always had a special appeal. The compulsion to garden, to control or imitate nature, to create an earthly paradise, has been with us from the beginning of civilisation. Our garden heritage is a rich tapestry of interwoven influences and ideas, but the recognition of its importance has been slow to develop. In the rush to discover and grow new plants, to develop new species and techniques, we were in danger of burying the gentle art of gardening under the science of horticulture. Only recently have historians acknowledged the artistic significance of gardens and practitioners become aware of the urgent need to conserve the parts of our garden heritage still extant.

Gardens are living, evolving creations and their care and conservation must evolve with them. The conservation of gardens is a complex process and bears little comparison to conservation in other areas. Gardens are usually preserved primarily for active use, for recreation, but their upkeep has changed with changes in the cost of labour and the availability of machinery, and they go on growing! Like buildings, gardens are conserved to be used; unlike buildings, they are not static. Only the built elements of a garden are static, and it is seldom appropriate to conserve only these elements of a design. The interest and the pleasure lie in the living and growing elements. How often has colour been quoted as the excuse for uniform planting in a parterre! It may be a mistaken method of providing interest, but the recognition, indeed tacit acceptance, of the essential ingredient of the planted element

Preface

is there. Gardens exist for the pleasure of the appreciation of nature through the growing of plants – that is their essence.

The history of garden design, as of other arts, borrows from different countries, the lead being taken first by one and then another. At present there is a tendency to look to England as leading the movement in garden conservation, and in England it was in fact suggested that this book should concentrate on garden conservation in England with conservation elsewhere covered in a subsequent volume. For a Scot based in Scotland that suggestion was hard to swallow! Just as the development of the landscape garden was not a phenomenon exclusive to England, neither is the development of conservation. The interest in a natural landscape style in the eighteenth century left England with a rich heritage of parks and gardens which has stimulated a growing concern with garden conservation, but the problems faced are common to all, and cross national boundaries. It is time for international co-operation, time to tackle problems in a broader context. In the preparation of this book limitations on time and resources have prevented the net from being cast further afield than Europe and America, but it is to be hoped that its scope is sufficiently wide to make it of assistance to those facing similar problems in other countries. Although all the gardens in the case studies belong to temperate climates the problems illustrated cover the care of plants in extremes of cold and drought, and the process of planning and managing the conservation of a garden has a universal application. It is only the balance of maintenance and control that may vary, whether in containing the luxuriant growth of plants in tropical climates or in nurturing the growth of less hardy plants in regions with cold winters.

The principles involved in garden conservation are relevant to all heritage gardens, but the clarity with which they can be expressed is hampered by the lack of universal agreement on the use of conservation terminology with regard to gardens. The 1981 ICOMOS Charter of Florence drafted some definitions, but was limited in its scope. Terminology still varies wildly from country to country, and definitions of terms should form the preamble to any literature or discussion paper if it is to be internationally understood. For the purpose of this book therefore the main terms are defined in the glossary which follows. They are explored more fully in Chapter 2 which deals with the problems involved in restoration.

Since this book is about the conservation of existing gardens, rather than the design and layout of new ones, few plans have been included, except where they are deemed an essential illustration to the text. There is no substitute for a visit to a garden if its nature is to be properly understood but, on the whole, photographs illustrate the character of a garden better than a two-dimensional plan.

Acknowledgements

I am deeply grateful both for the direct assistance which so many have contributed to the production of this book, and also for the indirect support and encouragement of friends and family which made the writing of it possible. My thanks go to them all, but in particular I wish to acknowledge and thank the following:

Ali O'Neale for permission to publish Iain's poem; His Grace the Duke of Atholl and Sir John Clerk of Penicuik for the use of material from family papers; Peter Goodchild of the Centre for the Conservation of Historic Parks and Gardens, York; John Dyke of the Centre for Environmental Interpretation; David Jacques of English Heritage; Dr Carla Oldenburger-Ebbers, Landbouwuniversiteit, Wageningen; Nora Mitchell of the US National Park Service; Mlle Monique Mosser; John Sales of the National Trust; Dr Erika Schmidt of the Institut für Grünplanung und Gartenarchitektur, Hannover; Dipl.-Ing. Stefan Rhotert, Bayerische Verwaltung der Staatlichen Schlösser; Dipl.-Ing. Hubert Wertz, Oberfinanzdirektion Karlsruhe; Dr Hans-Georg Preißel and Ronald Clark, Herrenhäuser Gärten; Dr Wilfried Hansmann, Landeskonservator Rheinland; M. Gilbert Vahé, Giverny; M. Olivier Choppin de Janvry of the Societé Civile du Désert de Retz; Janie Burford, Mavis Collier and Bill Tomlins of Painshill Park Trust; Julian Gibbs of the National Trust; Peter Hatch, Monticello; Bill Alexander, Biltmore Estate; Christopher Dingwall and James Simpson, my colleagues on the Hercules Garden project; Dean Norton, Mount Vernon; Gordon Chapel, Colonial Williamsburg; the Castle Bromwich Garden Trust; Pierre and Maud Dupas; Dirk and Eugenie van Weede; Robert and Norma Worden; and last, but above all, Paul Walshe and Jim Henderson, not only for the trouble they took to read and comment on the manuscript in draft, but also for their interest and sometimes teasing encouragement from the very beginning.

Acknowledgements

I am also indebted to the following for kind permission to reproduce copyright material:

Douglas Dunn for the quotation from his poem '75°', in *Northlight* (Faber & Faber, 1988); Brendan Kennelly for the quotation from his poem 'A Half-Finished Garden'; the controller of Her Majesty's Stationery Office for permission to reproduce part of a photograph of the Hercules Garden at Blair Castle; and the Royal Commission on the Ancient and Historical Monuments of Scotland for permission to reproduce a photograph of the painting of Yester House and gardens from the south by James de Witt.

Glossary

garden	an area of ground designed or laid out primarily to be used for pleasure, where the growing of plants is, or was, an important element.
heritage garden	a garden which, because of its historical, cultural or artistic attributes, can be regarded as being of local, regional, national or international significance.
to preserve	to keep intact, to keep from decay.
to conserve	to maintain in a safe or sound state.
to restore	to put back into an original state.
to reconstruct	to put back into the original form, or a replica of the original form.
to re-create	to create or form anew.

From the above definitions it will be understood that conservation, rather than preservation, is used as the overall, blanket term for the restoration, care and upkeep of gardens.

Background 1

Le monde se découvrant comme un jardin, le jardin se doit
d'enfermer le monde.

Jurgis Baltrusantis

The garden heritage – source and significance

Gardens are a vital part of our national and international heritage,
encompassing more facets of our cultural and social history than any
other art form. Many provide the settings for historic houses, others
are of interest in their own right. They are both a recreational and an
educational resource and are increasingly being recognised worldwide
as important national assets.

Gardens have always marked the development of civilisation. Their
proliferation reflects material prosperity, their design and creation the
tastes and interests of their period and cultural tradition. No study of
the Italian Renaissance would be complete without an understanding
of the significance of the garden within the Renaissance ideal, both as
a background to a cultured life and as an expression of the balance and
harmony between man and nature. The great French gardens of the
seventeenth century were the ultimate expression of the power and
wealth of their owners; their decay and neglect after the Revolution
reflected political change and the downfall of the aristocracy. Indeed,
to a large extent, interest in gardens and gardening in France died
with the Revolution, little being written on French gardens in French
thereafter, and only recently has there been a revival of general interest
among the French public.

On the one hand, gardens are our most accessible art form, but on the
other, the form in which it is most difficult to interpret the original
intentions of the designer. They can be enjoyed on many levels, from

the simple enjoyment of being outdoors in a pleasant environment, to an appreciation of their plants, or of their design and history, but, by their very nature, gardens are ephemeral. Most represent an overlapping kaleidoscope of change, through the seasons, through the growth, decay and renewal of their plant material and through the changes wrought by successive owners or designers. Yet they are arguably one of the best sources for the social historian, embodying, as they do, so many different elements, the art of the designer, the skills of craftsmen and gardeners, the cultural and social status of the owner.

If the conservation of our garden heritage is to be successful, it is essential to be clear about its purpose. Unlike archaeology, garden restoration can never be an exact science. Too much depends on transient elements, so that it is a continuing process, requiring constant adjustment and upkeep. A large part of its aim must be the enjoyment of users today, but we also owe to future generations the conservation of an important artistic and historic resource. Decisions about whether to conserve, restore or reconstruct must be taken within a historic and national or cultural context.

Historic development

The art of garden design has always borrowed from different periods and countries, but although historic influences cross national borders, separate gardening traditions developed within distinct geographic and cultural boundaries. For example, the English landscape style was only practised on a minor scale in Scotland, to whose more dramatic natural topography it was unsuited, and where, perhaps owing much to the customary excellence and practical ability of Scottish gardeners, as well as a natural conservatism, a formal gardening tradition continued, particularly in the immediate environs of the house. In America the English landscape style made most impact within the great American park movement, since it was land in public rather than private ownership that lent itself to the grand scale of an informal landscape.

On the continent the fashion for the 'English garden' led to the sweeping away of many of the more grandiose, high maintenance, formal schemes, although some of the built elements of the formal layout would often remain in uneasy alliance with the new informal landscape as in the Medici garden at Pratolino in Italy. In other places an 'English garden' was added to the side of a formal layout, as at Schwetzingen in Germany, where an eclectic range of garden features married the formal to the informal in a way that led eventually to the mockery of the 'jardin anglais'[1] by English travellers abroad. At its best, for example in the

1 'Il colosso dell'Appennino' in the Medici garden at Pratolino

park at Marly, Paris, now known as the Désert de Retz, with its twenty garden buildings related in a landscape setting, a combination of influences from two very different informal styles, the English and the Chinese, led to the emergence of the style known as 'anglo-chinois'.

Conservation of heritage gardens in Europe and America is usually concerned with those created since the Renaissance. On the whole, conservation applied to pre-medieval gardens is meaningless; they belong to the realm of archaeology. But the Renaissance garden looks back to the classical authors for its inspiration, to Homer and the 'Elysian fields', and to its immediate predecessor, the medieval garden, whose form and symbolism reflect the Persian 'paradise' or enclosed garden.

Early gardens were enclosed by a fence or wall, or terraced, in either case the boundary being clearly defined, separating the cultivated garden from encroaching nature, whether that meant the desert to the great early civilisations of Mesopotamia and Egypt, or wandering livestock to the medieval monastic community. The medieval enclosed garden represented both the earthly paradise of biblical times, the Garden of Eden and the garden of love portrayed in the Song of Songs, and also a celestial or spiritual paradise. The imagery of the Song of Songs, the garden as the bride, was combined with the Marian interpretation of the garden as the Virgin Mary with Christ as the gardener.

Such enclosed gardens existed not only within the monastery walls, but also within the defensive walls of medieval castles. The garden at Edzell in Kincardineshire, Scotland, survives as a late example of a castle garden on this scale. Although the planting is a creation of the 1930s, it was built in 1604 within the space bounded by the old moat, and is surrounded on three sides by defensive walls which are decorated with niches. The medieval castle of Trequanda in Tuscany, dating from the twelfth century, also contains a garden in the triangular space between its outer defensive and inner walls, although whether it was always planted as a garden is uncertain. The locals know the garden as the 'Bosco inglese', which suggests that it owes its current form to the Victorian revival of interest in Italian gardens.

Whereas the humanist gardens of the early Italian Renaissance were still walled or terraced, they were no longer secluded from the outside world, but rather embraced the view and the advantages of an elevated site. The importance of the view, the choice of site, and its integration with the landscape relate back to Roman descriptions of gardens, and also forward to the writings of the eighteenth century, such as the unpublished poem 'The Country Seat', by Sir John Clerk of Penicuik, describing the ideal siting and design for a country residence, and

2 The castle garden at Edzell whose decorated walls date from 1604

3 The 'Bosco inglese' of the medieval castle at Trequanda

Alexander Pope's 'Epistle to Lord Burlington' which advocated the encouragement of the 'spirit of the place'. Leon Battista Alberti's *De re aedificatoria,* explaining how a country house and its gardens should be planned, based on the writings of Pliny and written between 1450 and Alberti's death in 1472, was well known and widely influential even before it was printed in 1485. The small garden of the Palazzo Piccolomini in Pienza, built in 1459, is typical of the transition in garden design of this period. It is in effect an outdoor garden room to one side of the palace, with arched openings in the boundary hedge for the view.

The simplicity of these garden rooms was suited to the hilly Tuscan countryside and to Tuscan taste, more subtle than its Roman counterpart, so that the creation of this type of garden continued for longer in Tuscany than elsewhere. The garden of the Villa Capponi at Acetri, which dates from the second half of the sixteenth century, has three original 'rooms', a grassed terrace at the back of the house giving a view of Florence and the Arno from one end, a lemon garden opening off the other end, and a walled garden with windows, which was originally entered only through an underground passage from the house. The garden of the Villa Gamberaia, Settignano, is a typical Tuscan gem. Founded in 1610, although it probably assumed its present form in 1717, the villa is approached along a cypress walk. On the west of the villa is a grassed terrace with a magnificent view of Florence. To the south is a parterre garden, now a water garden but still retaining the traditional Renaissance layout of four parterres divided by paths, with a fountain in the circular space at the crossing. The bowling green runs the length of the grounds on the east. A small giardino segreto opens off the centre of it, with a lemon garden and a shady bosco above and to either side. Water is ducted into a grotto framed by cypress trees at one end of the bowling green. The other end is balustraded and overlooks the valley of the Arno and the olive groves, which come right up to the garden wall.

The siting and the planting were the most important elements in the design of Renaissance gardens in Tuscany; the architectural element was incidental. Two Medici gardens, however, were exceptions to this rule, the Boboli and Pratolino. These had a definite architectural form like the great Roman gardens, an extension of architecture into the landscape. The Boboli gardens survived the ravages of the English landscape style, probably because the plan is so well related to the topography of the site. The gardens were for public rather than private entertainment, and in the early seventeenth century, the addition of tiers of seats around an open space used for pageants revived the classical relationship between the theatre and garden design.

4   The garden 'room' of the
Palazzo Piccolomini, Pienza

5   Villa Capponi from the lemon
garden

The great water garden of the Villa d'Este at Tivoli, commissioned from Piero Ligorio in 1550 and completed in the 1580s, is considered to be the most typical example of a Roman High Renaissance garden. The full effect of the rising terraces and the splendid variety of water features must be viewed from the foot, but at each level there is spectacle, not only in the jets and fountains, grottos and water channels, but also in the vista across the Campagna. The Villa Lante at Bagnaia was designed by Vignola in 1564, and beautifully restored in 1954, since when it has won a well deserved reputation as the best kept garden in public ownership in Italy. It has a similar 'feel' to a Tuscan garden owing to its more intimate scale, but the use of water is entirely in the Roman tradition, although it is less flamboyant than at the Villa d'Este, making a play of the constant gentle movement of water along a central axis which recalls the Moorish gardens of southern Spain. The villa is divided into two parts and set halfway up the slope, on either side of the main axis, giving an unrivalled unity to the architectural composition of the garden. The prospect from the garden overlooks the rooftops of the borgo of Bagnaia in the foreground, and the central axis of the piazza meets that of the garden at the main entrance gate. This relationship between the village and the main approach to the villa was exploited by François Mansart in the siting of the French château of Balleroy, built in the 1620s, where the village street became an extension of the axis of the château.

The interplay of light and shade created by evergreen planting, the cooling effects of water, and the interest provided by stone sculpture and architectural details are the essence of the Italian Renaissance garden. The importance of shade, or the want of it, is highlighted in the restoration of the Medici garden at Castello. The lunette, painted by Giusto Utens between 1599 and 1602, depicts a central bosco around a circular pool. The replanting of this feature would have mitigated the current lack of charm about the garden by putting back the vertical accent, as well as giving an essential element of shade in a very flat, open space.

Although the shade of a bosco or planted walks was a vital part of the Italian garden, the more formal or architectural elements, in particular the parterre, were planned nearest the house. The parterre was intended to be viewed from above. Renaissance designs were geometrical, unlike the curving forms of the later French 'broderie', and laid out with evergreen herbs. Box was not widely used until after 1600 when its more enduring, if not endearing, qualities (its smell was unpopular) were found useful in forming the more intricate French designs. A fine example of a parterre dating from the end of the sixteenth century still exists at the Villa Ruspoli at Vignanello. The design is close to examples

6   One of the terraces of the water garden of Villa d'Este, Tivoli

7   The cascade on the central axis of the Villa Lante, Bagnaia

8   The château at Balleroy which dominates the axis of the village street

in Sebastiano Serlio's treatise *Architettura*, printed in 1537. It was laid out by Ottavia Orsini, and her initials are incorporated into the design of the central bed near the castle. It was originally planted in rosemary, but replanted in box early this century.

In spite of the fact that a combination of various evergreens made up the basic structure of planting in these Italian gardens, the planting of flowers played a much greater part than is generally realised. The parterre pattern was usually of simple geometrically-shaped beds in order to display the flowers. The Medici family introduced many new plants to their gardens, and the layouts of the beds used to display their collections can be seen in Utens' lunettes. In 1545 the first botanic garden was founded in Padua, and by 1552 there were already 1,500 species cultivated in the garden. The garden still retains its original form, and even some of the sixteenth-century plants, within the circular boundary wall. Here the beds are edged with stone rather than herbs. The botanic garden also has fine examples of wrought iron, a decorative material typical of the Veneto, in the form of plants and flowers which once adorned the gate posts.

Italian Renaissance gardens were well known outside Italy. A visit to Italy was regarded as an essential part of the education of a gentleman. One such traveller, Fynes Moryson, wrote a detailed account of his travels through Europe, *An Itinerary*, published in 1617. He describes the gardens at Pratolino and Castello, and elaborates on the grottos, fountains and water-controlled automata. His description of Buontalenti's grotto at Castello amply illustrates the delight taken in 'giochi d'acqua' (water jokes) in this period, as well as showing that a guided tour round a garden is nothing new:

> Here in another Cave are divers Images of beasts of Marble, curiously wrought, namely of Elephants, Camels, Sheepe, Harts, Wolves, and many other beasts, admirable for the engravers worke. Here our guide slipped into a corner, which was only free from the fall of waters, and presently turning a cock powred upon us a shower of raine, and therewith did wet those that had most warily kept themselves from wetting at all the other fountains.

It was not only travellers, but also war, that spread the Italian influence in garden design. In 1495 the French king, Charles VIII, revived his claim to Naples and Sicily, and invaded Italy. The invasion was shortlived but Charles, impressed by the cultural riches of Italy, and particularly by the gardens of the Poggio Reale where he stayed in Florence, brought back Italian artists and craftsmen to work in France. The influence of Italian culture was strengthened by further Italian

9   'Divers Images of beasts of Marble' in Buontalenti's grotto at Castello

expeditions under Louis XII and Francis I, and by the marriage of Henri II to Catherine de Medici.

The engravings of Jacques Androuet du Cerceau's plans and drawings, printed in *Les Plus Excellents Bastiments de France* in 1576 and 1579, are the best available reference for the Renaissance garden in France. Dr Joachim Cavallo's early twentieth-century re-creation of the gardens at Villandry, in the sixteenth-century style, was based on designs from this source. Few French Renaissance gardens survive, but at Chenonceaux the gardens of Diane de Poitiers and Catherine de Medici still exist on either side of the main, northern approach to the château, which is built out into the river, with a two-storey gallery on the bridge continuing the axis into the park on the south bank. These gardens were known to the young Queen of Scots, Mary Stuart, since a festival was held at Chenonceaux for her and her husband, Francis II, in 1560.

Sloping sites for French gardens were rare; flat sites more usual. Terraced gardens on sloping ground survive from the early seventeenth century at Montjeu near Autun, and at Brécy near Bayeux. On flat ground the need for drainage led to the design of large garden canals, so that, typically, the French château was separated from its forecourt and gardens by flat expanses of water as at Villandry. The garden gradually developed as the climax of an axial approach to the château, the axis itself first terminating on a grotto or other feature within the gardens, but eventually extending into the countryside, with the château being central to the overall plan of the policies.

By the early seventeenth century the lead in garden design had moved from Italy to France, culminating in the grand formal gardens of the wealthy financiers and that of Louis XIV at Versailles. These great French gardens were formal in the sense of being the setting for formal occasions. The garden was no longer a series of outdoor rooms which might be used for private entertainment, but rather a vast space laid out to be seen, principally from the house, and as an elaborate, theatrical backdrop, a stage set for the guests. The main purpose of the garden was to display the wealth and power of the owner.

The gradual change to the concept of the formal garden as a unified plan, centred on the château, and the development of the principal element, the 'parterres de broderie', are described by various authors in the first half of the seventeenth century. Olivier de Serres, in his *Théâtre d'Agriculture et Mesnages des Champs* published in 1600, describes, for the first time, how the proportions of a parterre should be adjusted to allow for distortions of perspective. He states that the parterre is now usually of box, and includes designs for parterres at

10   Stone lion guarding one of the terraces at Brécy

X

Fontainebleau, Saint-Germain-en-Laye and the Tuileries by the King's gardener, Claude Mollet. An advance in parterre design, the introduction of curving forms and arabesques, is illustrated in *Traité du Jardinage*, of 1683, by Jacques Boyceau, who also advocates the need for an overall balance of proportion in the garden plan. The concept of the formal garden is summed up in André Mollet's *Jardin de Plaisir*, published in 1651 while he was working for Queen Christina of Sweden.

The most important exponent of the French formal garden was André Le Notre, who worked early in his career with his father, Jean Le Notre, at the Tuileries in Paris. The garden that most clearly demonstrated his talents was that of Vaux-le-Vicomte, built for the financier Nicholas Fouquet between 1656 and 1661, and restored by Lainé and Henri Duchêne at the very end of the nineteenth century, so that its basic form today is very close to that of its original conception. At Vaux, Le Notre worked in collaboration with the architect Le Vau and the artist Le Brun, the same team that Louis XIV later appropriated to work at Versailles.

In comparison with Italian gardens, the gardens of Vaux-le-Vicomte owe nothing to the site, which crosses the shallow valley of the River Aqueil. The ground was levelled to create an expansive sloping platform, with the river channelled into a monumental canal on the main transverse axis. The width of the garden is such that the château commands centre stage from any point. From the château the vista appears continuous, stretching into the woods on the far side of the valley. Architectural features terminate the cross-axes which extend into the bosquets on either side of the main open space. There is a harmony and unity of composition in the balance of the parterres, pools and other features, but its scale, the vast control of nature in the clipped box, pyramids of yew and regular lines of trees, leaves one in no doubt as to the importance and riches of the owner. It is little wonder that it roused the ire of Louis XIV. On 17 August 1661, by inviting Louis and his court to an extravagant reception in the finished gardens, possibly with a view to offering Vaux to the King, Nicholas Fouquet overplayed his hand. Less than three weeks later he was disgraced, arrested and imprisoned, but the envy of Louis was to result in the greater extravagance of the gardens of Versailles.

In contrast to Vaux, where the gardens were designed and laid out within five years, at Versailles the gardens evolved over fifty years, from the early 1660s until Louis' death in 1715. Louis himself wrote an itinerary for viewing the gardens, *La Manière de Montrer Les Jardins de Versailles*, first produced in 1689, but rewritten several times. The extent of Versailles was so vast that it would have taken most of a day to

11 The vista from the château across the expansive sloping platform of the gardens of Vaux-le-Vicomte

12 Versailles – the central axis from the Apollo basin

follow the full itinerary. So much land used purely as a pleasure ground was a conspicuous display of arrogance, reinforced by an extensive use of symbolism, of the sun-god Apollo equated with Louis himself. The main axis of the gardens follows the path of the sun, running east–west, from the château to the far end of the great canal. Versailles was primarily a water garden, but on such a scale that the water supply was scarcely adequate, despite the building of the 'machine de Marly' in the 1680s, which pumped water from the Seine, and the fountains were played in sequential groups as the visitors progressed round the garden. Today the supply of water to the fountains is restricted to certain days in the year.

The gardens at Versailles were used extensively for royal festivities and entertainments, and flowers were planted temporarily in the bosquets for special occasions. Bedding out could thus be said to be the French method of flower gardening. This was especially true at Trianon, another of Louis' gardens, created for his mistress, where, in an exception to the general rule, the parterres were made with flowers instead of box and coloured earth. The flowers were planted out so that they could be changed easily, and as often as required.

In a garden designed, like Versailles, principally to impress, a degree of maturity in the planting was necessary from the outset. Louis employed one man, Octavien Henry, between 1671 and 1680, whose primary responsibility was to find and transplant shrubs and trees, some of them very large. Thousands of shrubs and trees from the nurseries at Vaux were moved to the royal gardens. Hornbeam hedges were commonly used, and avenues were planted with elm or, increasingly, with horse chestnut. The practice of lining the allées of the bosquets with one species of tree gave way to the planting of rows of cut yew and box in front of clipped hornbeam. After the mid-1670s, trellis made of sweet chestnut, painted green, and covered with climbing plants, began to replace hedges.

The creation of these grand gardens was on a scale comparable to a labour intensive industry today. They offered employment for hundreds, both skilled and unskilled, in their setting out and their maintenance, but they cost so much to run that, after the death of their owners, and with them their ostentatious raison d'être, they often fell into disrepair. Nevertheless the French owe much to this period of their garden heritage, even where the gardens as such no longer exist. The main lines of the Tuileries became the basis of Haussman's plan for Paris in the nineteenth century. The central allée is now the Champs-Elysées.

The prodigious display of wealth in large tracts of land used solely as pleasure grounds, with no complementary productive or agricultural use, was not something that could be long sustained, particularly since the extravagance of Louis XIV had exhausted the French coffers, and continuing war and excessive taxation during the eighteenth century reduced the wealth of the French nobility. The great French formal garden held sway for a comparatively short time before the advent of the fashion for the 'natural' landscape, although its influence was important in the later return to the formal garden at the end of the nineteenth century.

In the Netherlands, although the French broderies crept into the parterre, the gardens remained very much four-square in plan with small canals, necessary for drainage, framing the garden boundaries. At Het Loo (the royal palace built by William III between 1684 and 1700, and subject to painstaking restoration since 1975), the gardens, although they strove to rival Versailles, were divided into small garden beds even in the parts of the garden distant from the palace. Dutch gardens were always productive, and the small garden bed was best suited to the display and cultivation of plants. An increase in plant collecting and the raising of new cultivars paralleled the rise of the science of botany during the seventeenth century. Lavish plantings of tulips were a characteristic of larger Dutch gardens. Tulip mania had swept across Europe in the early years of the century, and although it peaked shortly before 1637 when the market collapsed, books such as John Parkinson's *Paradisi in sole Paradisus terrestris* of 1629, which praised the tulip as 'above and beyond' all other flowers, were long influential.

Both French and Dutch influences can be traced in gardens throughout Europe around the turn of the seventeenth century. Many French gardeners worked in Germany. In 1682 Martin Charbonnier started to design the Electress Sophie's gardens at Herrenhausen in Hanover, but here the boundary canals are Dutch in form as they are at Schleissheim in Munich, the work of another Frenchman, Dominique Girard. Both gardens are extant. At Herrenhausen the parterres disappeared under lawn and new plantings of exotic trees and shrubs were made in the nineteenth century. Neglect and then devastation during the Second World War have prompted two restorations since the city of Hanover took over the gardens in 1935, and in the 1960s a more comprehensive effort to restore the gardens to their original layout was initiated. At Schleissheim the landscape design of von Sckell in 1801 avoided alterations to the parterres, which survive intact. Girard also worked with François Curvillié at the Augustusberg in Brühl, rescued in the 1930s from the 'English garden' by P. J. Lenné which replaced it in the late eighteenth century, restored to its 1750 plan, and recently the subject of a further conservation project.

With the accession of William and Mary to the thrones of England and Scotland, the reputation of the University of Leiden, with its Hortus Publicus, as a European centre of learning, including botany, where many a Scottish gentleman completed a legal or medical education, and the accessibility of the Netherlands to the traveller, it was inevitable that the French influence on garden design should be tempered by the Dutch. At Hampton Court, William and Mary had large formal gardens laid out with parterres of broderie. The broderie, however, lasted only twenty years before Queen Anne had it removed because she disliked the smell of box. At Hampton Court today the bones of the formal plan survive together with the original yews, now overgrown and incongruous, rigid pyramids on stalks. Current debate centres on whether or not they should be retained.

The garden at Westbury Court, Gloucestershire, the subject of an early 1970s restoration by the National Trust, is a rare example of a small garden with canals and pavilion in the Dutch manner. Its site, on the water meadows of the River Severn, is not dissimilar to the flat, watery landscape of the Netherlands. The main canal, its flanking hedges with topiary pyramids and balls of yew and holly, the pavilion and parterre near the house, shown in Kip's engraving, are well documented and were built by Maynard Colchester between 1696 and 1705. The second canal, in its present T-shape form, was probably added by his nephew after 1715, together with the walled garden and summerhouse.

Formal gardens in the Italian Renaissance tradition continued to be created alongside those which emulated French or Dutch examples. In Scotland, near Hamilton, the small hanging garden of Barncluith, whose terraces are now sadly neglected and vandalised, has been described as Dutch, but this is indicative of a contemporary perception of topiary as a Dutch feature, since the hanging terraces can hardly be interpreted as having a Dutch precedent. John Macky, writing in 1725, describes,

> a very romantick garden called Baroncleuh, which consists of seven
> hanging terras-walks, down to a riverside. In some of these walks
> are banquetting houses with walks and grottos, and all of them fill'd
> with large evergreens, in the shape of beasts and birds.

Instructions for building the retaining walls for such terrace walks are included in the first Scottish gardening book, *The Scots Gard'ner* by John Reid, published in Edinburgh in 1683. Reid emigrated to America the same year, but his book, written 'for the climate of Scotland', contains invaluable information about the design and cultivation of the seventeenth-century Scottish garden.

13   The pavilion fronting the end of the main canal in the garden at Westbury Court

The form of the Great Garden at Pitmedden in Aberdeenshire, with its belvedere, the steps descending from the upper level, and the small garden pavilions in the southwest and northwest corners, recalls Utens' lunette depicting the Medici garden of La Petraia. Sir Alexander Seton founded the garden in 1675. The National Trust for Scotland, which now owns Pitmedden and was responsible for the re-creation of the garden within its walls in the 1950s, attributes a French influence to the design through Sir Alexander's acquaintance with Sir William Bruce, and through him to the work of Le Notre – a tenuous link at best, and a theory which is not supported by the enclosed nature of the garden. It is more likely that Sir Alexander drew his inspiration from the gardens of Yester House and Pinkie, both belonging to the Winton branch of his family and situated in the county of East Lothian where he spent his boyhood. The gardens at Yester were well recorded by James de Witt in paintings executed before 1685, and the large formal garden of Pinkie House, Musselburgh, was described by Sir John Lauder of Fountainhall in his journals written between 1665 and 1676,

> A most sweit garden, the knot much larger than at Hamilton and in better order. The rest of the yeard nether so great nor in so good order nor so well planted with varietie as is Hamilton yeards. The knot heir will be 200 foot square, a mighty long grein walk. Saw figs at verie great perfection...
> 18 plots in the garden with a summer house and sundry pondes.

These and other examples of the smaller formal garden in the Italian tradition were not only created, but survived, for longer in Scotland because they were better suited both to the topography, and to the social mores of the Scottish people. They serve as invaluable reference points for the formal garden in Europe. Furthermore, in Scotland the development from the formal to the landscape style can be observed in microcosm in gardens still extant, whereas in England greater wealth enabled more sweeping changes which left little of the older garden landscape untouched.

The development of the country house in Scotland was a phenomenon which dates from the Restoration in 1660. Perhaps the first well-known garden designer in Scotland was Sir William Bruce who, having travelled extensively in France, returned to translate the French use of the long axial vista into a Scottish context by using natural features to terminate a central axis, thus bringing the wider landscape into the garden as an integral part of the design. At Balcaskie, Fife, where in 1665 he constructed a terraced garden on three levels to the south of the altered castle, Bruce centred the view on the Bass Rock, and at Kinross House, built in the 1680s, Loch Leven Castle became the foil to the design.

14 Painting of Yester House and gardens from the south by James de Witt (pre-1685). Photograph courtesy
of the RCAHMS

Following the Act of Union in 1707 there was a distinct shift in the Scottish social climate, a new breed of anglophile among the Scottish gentry. This was exemplified in the person of Sir John Clerk of Penicuik who, with William Adam as his architect, created the small estate of Mavisbank at Loanhead near Edinburgh in order to house his collection of paintings and sculpture and as a place to entertain his friends. His poem 'The Country Seat' was written in English rather than the Scottish vernacular. In form it borrows from the Dutch literary genre of the poem in praise of the country residence, with which Clerk must have been familiar since he studied in Leiden. It also reflects the early eighteenth-century revival of interest in the principles of the classical authors in relation to the villa garden. In the introduction to the poem Clerk justifies his writing in verse by reference to Virgil's *Georgics*. Clerk's poem was written in 1727, and undoubtedly reflects his work at Mavisbank which was begun in 1723. In it Clerk extols the virtue of choosing a site where nature is conducive to the design,

> The darling Country Seat must only be
> Where good and Bounteous Nature seems inclined
> By moderate culture to reward our Pains;

This sentiment corresponds with that which Alexander Pope expressed in his 'Epistle to Lord Burlington' of 1731 with a plea to follow nature and respect the *genius loci* (spirit of the place). The seeds of the new appreciation of the natural in garden design were set by the ridicule of the fashion for topiary, first by Joseph Addison in the *Spectator* in 1712, and then by Pope in his satirical list of topiary figures for sale in the *Guardian* in 1713, and reinforced by Switzer in his *Ichnographia Rustica* of 1718, where he advocated that the whole estate should be both beautiful and productive. Nevertheless it should not be thought that the merging of garden and landscape was a process that happened in a few short years. Serpentine walks crept but slowly into garden plans, and it was a long time before the formal outlines of straight avenues disappeared.

The main feature of Clerk's design at Mavisbank was the three straight avenues radiating from the house, across the slope of the north bank of the River North Esk. A long canal, its outlines now obscured by a later attempt to achieve a 'natural' pond, occupied part of the main central avenue, and in 1737 a doocot was built to terminate the vista. The house faces east and is set in front of an ancient earthwork. On the south side is a wilderness area, below which were two walled gardens, one circular and one rectangular, of which only the circular one survives, in a modified form, owing to the construction of a weir which altered the course of the river. Clerk carried out much planting

15   The parterre at Chatelherault, replanted to a pattern revealed by archaeological investigation

both here and at Penicuik, and his unpublished notes, 'Memorandum concerning the planting of Trees for the climat of Pennycook', give fascinating insights into his methods of cultivation. The willingness of the district council and local trusts to rescue Mavisbank from long neglect and deliberate vandalism has so far been hampered by problems of ownership and lack of finance, but it is to be hoped that Edinburgh's new 'Greenbelt Initiative' will enable the start of a restoration programme.

Clerk's early patronage of William Adam exerted considerable influence on the architect's development as a landscape designer. In 1727 Adam joined Clerk on a visit to London where they saw work in progress on Lord Burlington's villa at Chiswick. Burlington was at the centre of the classical revival. His gardens at Chiswick imitated ideas from Pliny's villa gardens to provide a suitable setting for the Paladian villa, and in 1728 he sponsored the publication of Robert Castell's *Villas of the Ancients*. Thus, through Clerk, Adam was first introduced to contemporary intellectual thought on garden design. In his work, Adam's own expressed penchant for the informal is constrained by his skilful adaptation to the often more conservative wishes of his patrons. Adam's schemes demonstrate a wide stylistic vocabulary. His plan for the Dun landscape bears striking similarities to a plate in Switzer's *Ichnographia Rustica*. At Newliston House, West Lothian, the bastion walls and the sequence of canals, taking advantage of the gently sloping site, have Dutch precedents, and it is known that in 1726, the date attributed to the original plan, Adam visited the Low Countries. The plan contains formal Baroque features, the groves or wildernesses in compartments with their cabinets, their radiating walks on diagonal axes or in the star pattern, and, only on the periphery, a serpentine walk. The type of planting employed in such a design was detailed by Batty Langley in his *New Principles of Gardening*, published in 1728, followed in 1731 by the first edition of Philip Miller's influential work, the *Gardeners' Dictionary*.

At Chatelherault, the hunting lodge that Adam built for the Duke of Hamilton in the 1730s, the formal approach along a double avenue from Hamilton Palace was in complete contrast to the natural scenery of the gorge behind. Hamilton Palace was demolished in 1927 but, thanks to the co-operation of the district councils and the Scottish Development Department, and grants from the National Heritage Memorial Fund, Chatelherault has recently been restored and the avenue and parterre replanted.

The key to understanding the juxtaposition of the formal and the natural in the early landscape designs of the eighteenth century is that designers sought the enhancement of nature, rather than its rigid control as represented at Versailles. (Indeed in England, though not in Scotland, the informal was equated with British political freedom, and the Gothic temple of Liberty at Stowe was a monument to that effect.) It is this aim which gradually led in England to the point where park and garden were indistinguishable, flowers were eliminated, and the productive element hidden behind a wall and banished from the immediate vicinity of the house. This integration of garden and park was made possible by the device of a ha-ha, a sunken ditch which acts as a barrier to livestock, but promotes the illusion of a continuous greensward. The first ha-has were probably at Blenheim, in 1712, and at Stowe, where Charles Bridgeman was working from 1713.

The early decades of the eighteenth century saw the beginnings of a cultural flowering in which interest in Italy and the interpretation of classical landscapes as seen in the work of Italian painters, such as Claude Lorrain, Gaspard Poussin and Salvator Rosa, led to a much more three-dimensional approach to the landscape, and where often the designed landscape itself attempted to emulate the epic poem. It was not until this century and the work of Gertrude Jekyll in her colour borders that the roles of painter and gardener were again so closely related. As early as 1705 Vanbrugh had expressed the wish for a landscape painter to design the landscape at Blenheim, but it was William Kent in the 1730s who first applied the painter's eye to the landscape garden, seeing it as a series of scenes, perhaps best demonstrated in his work at Rousham in Oxfordshire (although he worked at many of the well-known gardens of the century, at Chiswick, Stowe and Claremont). Presumably Sir John Clerk had applied much the same technique to the landscape at Mavisbank. Despite a wealth of information in family papers, no plan exists, except of the forecourt between the two wings of the house. By contrast, the designs of William Adam sometimes read better on paper than on the ground. At Taymouth, for example, it seems highly improbable that the avenues shown on the plan would ever have been planted on the steep hillsides before and behind the house. Above all, the eighteenth century was the age of the amateur in landscape design although the professional was still employed for the various garden buildings which formed incidents in the landscape, either isolated as at Castle Howard, Yorkshire, or connected by a walk as at Stourhead, Wiltshire.

Stourhead was the work of the banker Henry Hoare (1705–85) and his grandson, Sir Richard Colt Hoare. The main garden buildings were designed by the architect Henry Flitcroft, and all were complete by 1783 when Sir Richard added the gravel paths. The planting of exotics in his time, and into the nineteenth century, has changed the character of the vegetation, but the layout retains the spirit of Henry Hoare's original concept. The garden unfolds in a series of scenes reminiscent of a Claudian landscape, with the various garden buildings glimpsed across a lake. An itinerary was suggested to the visitor and inscriptions alluded to Virgil's *Aeneid*. Since its early days Stourhead has been much visited, and the National Trust has sought to reconcile the conflicting interests of visitors with those of conservation in its 1978 restoration proposals.

The work of William Shenstone at the Leasowes, Shropshire, often described as an ideal example of the 'ferme ornée', was less enduring, indeed barely surviving forty years beyond his death in 1763, but it was no less admired in its time. Its importance and influence depended on its concept as a landscape garden. Shenstone's modest means did not enable him to create grand or permanent garden features; today the outlines can be traced but the details have gone. In his *Unconnected Thoughts on Gardening*, printed after his death in 1764, Shenstone expresses the thought that a garden might resemble a dramatic poem. He sees landscape gardening as an extension of the art of painting, and divides 'landskips' into three types: the 'sublime' which includes the most rugged scenes; the 'beautiful', gentler and more regular; and the 'melancholy' which is often connected with a ruin. All, in his estimation, are necessary to illustrate the variety in nature which is essential to a complete composition, and his theories were put into practice in the walk round the Leasowes, where seats and sometimes inscriptions dictated where the visitor should pause to view the scene.

One of the most striking incorporations of a ruin into the landscape garden was that at Studley Royal in Yorkshire, where in 1768 the grounds were extended to include Fountains Abbey, as had apparently been the original intention of the owner, John Aislabie, when he first started his improvements in the 1720s. The site is now on the World Heritage List, and the co-operation of the Department of the Environment and the National Trust, with the help of professional consultants, has resulted in a fifteen-year plan for its restoration. At Painshill, the work of yet another amateur, Charles Hamilton, between 1738 and 1773, a massive restoration project run by a local trust has been under way since 1981. The variety of garden buildings, in particular the 'Gothic' abbey and temple and the grottos which were built of limestone tufa, together with the planting in which conifers predominate, evoke more of the spirit of Salvator Rosa's paintings than those of Claude in a 'wildness' which combines and extends Shenstone's 'sublime' and 'melancholic' and was to become much admired later in the century. A similar spirit pervades the recently rediscovered landscape at Hawkstone in Shropshire, where an imaginative approach to initiating a restoration project promises to overcome the difficulties of working

16 The lake, bridge and Pantheon at
Stourhead

17 View from the Gothic temple,
Painshill

with the twenty-two different owners of the site, to effect the rescue of a magnificent picturesque landscape. Sir Rowland Hill began to acquire the land in 1737 and most of the ornamental walks were completed between the 1740s and 1800. The first guide book was produced in 1783, and the Hill family were so successful in attracting visitors that the Hawkstone Inn became a hotel whence the guided walks started.

The most renowned landscape gardener of the second half of the eighteenth century was Lancelot Brown, dubbed 'Capability' because of his propensity for saying that a landscape had 'capabilities'. His work was ideally suited to the gently rolling contours of 'England's green and pleasant land'.[2] By respecting the natural lie of the land, and using clumps and belts of trees to emphasise and to disguise, Brown created one integrated, but varying, scene, usually around a lake made by damming the lower end of a river valley, and allowing the water to spread out along natural contours. The lake at Blenheim, where Brown worked from 1764 to 1774, is a typical example. By raising the water level he joined the two lakes either side of Vanbrugh's bridge. Tree planting and the curve of the shore conceal the boundaries of the lake to create the illusion of a wide flowing river. Here too the original formal gardens by Vanbrugh, London and Wise, and Bridgeman were destroyed in favour of a characteristic expanse of grass in front of the house. The loss of trees through Dutch elm disease, beech bark disease and drought and the consequent need for replanting has prompted, at the instigation of the Countryside Commission, the adoption of a restoration plan devised for the estate by Cobham Resource Consultants and Hal Moggridge, in which the Brownian aspects of the landscape will be conserved.

Brown used, besides the cedar of Lebanon, only native trees in his work so that where later plantings of exotic trees have been added, distinct colour changes impinge unnaturally on the subtle shades of green. This is noticeable at Blenheim, where clumps or roundels of copper beech and of blue cedar were planted early this century. Criticism of Brown's work centred on the lack of definition between the designed landscape and the surrounding countryside, and yet this very factor was probably the most influential in increasing perception and appreciation of the natural landscape. It was not the tame naturalness of a Brownian landscape which was most admired however, but a naturalness of an altogether more wild and picturesque beauty. This admiration was explained by Edmund Burke in his *Philosophical Enquiry into the Origins of our Ideas of the Sublime and the Beautiful* in 1758, and later promoted by the Rev. William Gilpin's influential descriptions of 'picturesque' scenery in his published tours of the 1770s.[3] It led to an increasing interest in the Scottish landscape in particular at the end of the century, to which works like Robert Burns' 'The Humble Petition of the Bruar Water to the Noble Duke of Atholl', of 1787, pay tribute. Burns' plea,

> Would then my noble master please
> To grant my highest wishes?
> He'll shade my banks wi' tow'ring trees
> And bonie spreading bushes.

did not go unheeded, although planting was not begun until after Burns' death in 1796. Such efforts to enhance the natural landscape by planting may be seen as the forerunners of the plantsman's 'American' or woodland garden in the nineteenth and earlier twentieth centuries, especially typical of the west coast of Scotland where the climate is well suited to the growing of exotic species.

The picturesque scene was as often depicted by artists as by poets in the late eighteenth century. Travelling to view scenes of natural beauty like the Falls of Bruar became a fashionable thing to do, and the correct way to view such a scene was as a framed picture. Sometimes a mirror was carried for the purpose. In gardens the imitation of the 'wild' was carried to an ever more unnatural extreme in the proliferation of Gothic buildings, hermitages and grottos, rusticated temples and root and bone houses, the ideas for many of which can be found in Humphry Repton's *Theory and Practice of Landscape Gardening*, of 1803. These features were built as part of an attempt to achieve a total landscape, the idea broached by Shenstone.

Outside the mainstream of development from formal Baroque classicism to the 'natural' style, but bridging the gap was the Rococo style, a brief period in garden design of which, in England, only the paintings of Thomas Robins survive. One garden however, that of Painswick House in Gloucestershire, is being reconstructed from his painting of 1748. The greatest flowering of this style, at least in gardens still extant, was in Germany where the gardens at Weikersheim are a delightful example. Over fifty sculptures express movement and humour within a rectangular garden, quartered in the Renaissance tradition, in a way which is the antithesis of the severity of the grand Baroque manner. The style is characterised by decorative shell work, of which the shell gallery in the garden at Rozendaal near Arnhem is typical, by asymmetry and occasionally by Chinese buildings. Its lightheartedness contrasts with the gloom and grandeur of the picturesque.

The Chinese approach to the landscape garden was explored by Sir William Chambers in his *Dissertation on Oriental Gardening* in 1772, and Chambers' pagoda survives at Kew, but in eighteenth-century gardens in England examples of chinoiserie were confined to architecture. In Scotland the second Duke of Atholl's garden at Blair Castle presented a more complete picture, with views across the canal pond down the centre of the garden similar to scenes depicted on the Chinese porcelain and lacquered objects which the Duke collected, but it was on the Continent that the English and Chinese traditions combined best to express the idea of the total landscape. The Désert de Retz on the edge of the Royal Forest of Marly, built in the fifteen years preceding the French Revolution by François de Monville, originally contained twenty buildings linked only by their landscape setting. The Chinese house, the earliest of the buildings, now gone but recorded in drawings, was probably influenced by Chambers' *Designs of Chinese Buildings, Furniture, Dresses etc.* (1757), which was produced in a French edition by Le Rouge in 1776. It was surrounded by its own Chinese water garden. Of the other buildings, the ruined column also contained a house which influenced Jefferson in one of his first plans for the Capitol in Washington. It is destined to become a centre for the study of historic gardens as part of the current restoration scheme for the park.

Both Thomas Jefferson and George Washington were instrumental in introducing the natural style of landscape gardening to America. Washington's library contained copies of Batty Langley's *New Principles of Gardening* (1728) and of Philip Miller's *Gardeners' Dictionary* (1763 edition). At Mount Vernon the house takes advantage of the wide view of the Potomac River on one side, and a vista across the obligatory expanse of green into the countryside on the other. Serpentine paths approach the house with flanking wildernesses and groves to screen the plantations, but Washington's love of order shows in the symmetry of the plan. At Monticello Jefferson too laid out a serpentine path round a lawn in front of the house, but the main approach was on the other side. The siting of the house on a hilltop and the long terrace of the vegetable garden with its orchard below, through which the drive approaches, are reminiscent of a Tuscan farm, aptly reflecting the name of the estate. Jefferson had a training in surveying, was widely travelled and interested in all aspects of architecture and gardening and was often consulted on design matters by his friends. In America it was not until the mid-nineteenth century and the work of Andrew Jackson Downing that the professional made a significant contribution to landscape design.

In England the work of Humphry Repton, who started his career as a landscape gardener in 1788, was gradually leading the move away from the total simplicity of the Brownian landscape style and reintroducing a degree of formal gardening next to the house. Repton showed his design proposals through the persuasive medium of his 'Red Books'. A picture of the existing landscape, usually exaggerated, was changed, by

18 Detail of the shell gallery, recently restored, at Rosendaal

19 A dwarf caricature of the huntsman, one of the sculptures at Weikersheim

20 Buildings and plan of the Chinese garden at the Désert de Retz

the lifting of a flap, into one of the new landscape. Repton's work spanned the turn of the century and the shift of emphasis from park to garden, where flowers and even fountains were once again permissible. Although Repton's own return to the formal was limited, it was further accepted by W. S. Gilpin in his *Practical Hints for Landscape Gardening* in 1832. In 1828 Sir Walter Scott, with a decisiveness which smacks of his Scottish background, drew a distinction between the open, natural park, and the enclosed, ornamental garden in his essay 'On Ornamental Plantations and Landscape Gardening' in the *Quarterly Review*. This was to be taken further by Sir Robert Lorimer in his reflections on the traditional Scottish garden at the very end of the century. In his talk entitled 'On Scottish Gardens' given to the Edinburgh Architectural Association in 1898, Lorimer began,

> A garden is a sort of sanctuary, a chamber roofed by heaven
> To wander in, to cherish, to dream through undisturbed,
> A little pleasaunce of the soul, by whose wicket the world can be shut.

Several factors were important in the development of garden design from the 1830s onwards. Landscape and garden design had changed so much over the previous century that the reintroduction of the flower garden and a degree of formality encouraged a conscious reference to design precedents from the past and, later, the first efforts at historic recreation and restoration. Also, the rise in prosperity of the urban middle classes paralleled an interest in smaller gardens and a consequent proliferation of gardening books and manuals. The rapid introduction of hundreds of new species, particularly after the invention of the Wardian case which enabled safe transportation of plant material, together with the development of glasshouses, prompted new methods of growing and displaying plants, and finally, the care and character of the greensward was transformed by the invention of the lawnmower.

The most influential writer on gardening matters during the first half of the nineteenth century was the Scot, J. C. Loudon. His *Encyclopedia of Gardening* was first published in 1822, and in 1826 he produced the first issue of the *Gardener's Magazine*. His writings contain instructions for all the various garden elements which became fashionable during the nineteenth century: glasshouses, the fernery, rockery, shrubbery and rose garden, the practice of floriculture, and massed carpet bedding. Massed bedding displays were an innovation made possible by the introduction of suitable species of annuals and the development of hybrids. There were rules for combining different contrasting colours; only later in the century were tonal compositions deemed acceptable. The bedding out of annuals as it persists in Britain and on the Continent today was particularly suitable for providing colour in urban parks

21 Schloss Dyck, where Thomas Blaikie designed the 'English garden' early in the nineteenth century

22 Urn and topiary in the late nineteenth-century formal garden at Weldam

where industrial pollution was often so severe as to limit the number of trees and shrubs that could be grown to a few species. The practice of bedding out also lent itself to the planting of parterres in a formal manner. One of the most elaborate examples was that created at Drummond Castle, Perthshire, in the 1840s.

The Victorians were eclectic in their use of different garden styles. One of the most typical of the period was the Italianate style, in which the flower parterre, along with gravel walks, stonework, clipped hedges and topiary, was an important element. Many of these gardens were illustrated in Inigo Triggs' book *Formal Gardens in England and Scotland* in 1902. Italianate gardens were created on the continent also, and even re-exported by the English to Italy. The Castel del Poggio near Fiesole has an Italianate garden whose proportions betray its origins, and the garden at Weldam in Holland was designed by Edouard André in the formal manner at the end of the century. One of the finest examples of mixed styles in a Victorian garden is at Biddulph Grange in Staffordshire, where initiatives taken during the 1970s are finally resulting in restoration. Here, by the use of formal elements and of plants from different countries, an eclectic range of follies were given separate and appropriate settings. Notable amongst them are the Egyptian garden, where a topiary pyramid towers over the stone entrance, and the area known simply as 'China' which 'like China itself, is exceedingly difficult of access'[4] and contains a collection of Chinese plants. In providing individual settings for the buildings, this garden can be seen as progressing one stage further than the 'jardin anglo-chinois' of the previous century where the follies were related by, rather than directly to, the landscape.

Such was the variety of garden styles employed in the nineteenth century that it might be said that only the 'natural' landscape style was out of fashion. Landscape gardens were however designed for the display of exotic trees and shrubs. Early in the century the Scotsman, Thomas Blaikie, was employed at Schloss Dyck near Düsseldorf to design an 'English garden' for the display of a collection of rare trees and shrubs. In America the work of Frederick Law Olmsted, particularly in his designs for public parks, represents the culmination of the landscape movement. Towards the end of his career he was asked to lay out the grounds of Biltmore House, the Vanderbilt estate at Asheville, North Carolina. Olmsted's mastery of design showed in his landscape treatment of the approach road. One of the most spectacular parts of the gardens was the woodland area of the azalea garden, but an 'English Walled Garden' and an 'Italian Garden', adjacent to the house, were also included.

23   The gardens of Inverewe

Towards the end of the nineteenth century, and into the beginning of the twentieth century, three factors were most apparent in garden design. Plants were better appreciated for their form, colour and foliage and the contribution they could make to garden design. There was a return to the traditional Renaissance use of architecture as a framework to the garden, and there was an increasing interest in the historic garden.

William Robinson was the first to advocate that the qualities of the plants should influence their setting in his book, *The Wild Garden*, of 1870. Gertrude Jekyll accepted many of his precepts when describing the ideas that governed the development of her own garden at Munstead Wood in *Wood and Garden* in 1899. In France the painter Claude Monet's garden at Giverny, north west of Paris, was one where the plants themselves were of prime importance. In 1977 it was restored with reference to Monet's paintings, photographs, nurserymen's records and the recollections of friends and family. Many of the plant collectors were Scots, so it is not surprising that one of the best wild gardens created to display a plant collection to advantage was that of Inverewe, founded by Osgood Mackenzie in 1862 in magnificent surroundings on the edge of a sea loch in Ross and Cromarty. Since 1952 it has been in the care of the National Trust for Scotland.

The case for a return to Renaissance traditions was made by Sir Reginald Blomfield in his book, *The Formal Garden in England* in 1892. The creation of George Sitwell's garden at Renishaw in Derbyshire put Blomfield's principles into practice, and is described by his son, Sir Osbert Sitwell, in his autobiography. William Robinson seems to have been inclined to somewhat vitriolic attacks on his contemporaries, and launched into argument with Blomfield in *Garden Design and Architects' Gardens* the same year. Nonetheless, that the principles of the two men were not mutually exclusive was ably demonstrated by the partnership of Gertrude Jekyll with the architect, Sir Edwin Lutyens. The garden at Hidcote, the home of the American, Lawrence Johnston, from 1904, is an amateur creation in the same idiom, divided into different architectural compartments with the walls and hedges providing a foil for the planted borders. In Scotland, where the Renaissance tradition had always had a place, the gardens at Kellie Castle and Earlshall in Fife, among others, were re-created by Sir Robert Lorimer. At Kellie, Lord Crawford (1974) recalled a coherence of composition emphasised by the main east–west grass path bordered on each side by a uniform and predominantly white herbaceous planting backed with hollyhocks. There was the traditional Scottish mix of fruit, flowers and vegetables. Within the walled garden at Crathes Castle near Banchory the small gardens, surrounded by yew hedges dating from 1702, were an ideal setting for the display of an extensive collection of plants. An account

24   Hidcote – walls and hedges provide a foil for the planted borders

25   Herbaceous planting in the walled garden at Kellie Castle

of the garden was given by Gertrude Jekyll in *Some English Gardens* (2nd edition) in 1904.

In the 1880s the increasing interest in the historic garden and the formal tradition led to the first attempt at accurate restoration in the gardens of Vaux-le-Vicomte by Lainé and Henri Duchêne. From 1906 the gardens at Villandry were elaborately re-created in the sixteenth-century manner, using designs from du Cerceau's engravings, by Dr Joachim Cavallo. These were the beginnings of the stimulation of public interest which is vital to the conservation of gardens. In this century the Victorian tradition continues, with the main emphasis in garden design on plants and planting. Since the First World War labour has become increasingly expensive, so that the chief innovation within the planted elements has been the large-scale use of shrubs as ground cover to reduce maintenance. The one new departure has been sculpture gardens, where the display of sculpture is the prime objective, but perhaps the most important change this century is the recognition of the importance of the garden or landscape art form, not just in current practice, but more particularly in a historic context, and with it an increasing awareness of this most fragile part of our heritage.

The movement towards conservation

Changing attitudes to our garden heritage have been reflected worldwide in the incorporation of historic precedents into garden design, and in the appreciation of historic gardens, promoted first by individuals and private organisations, but increasingly by government and educational bodies, in moves to prevent their loss. As an educational resource, to all except the specialist, a historic garden is only as good as the clarity with which it is presented to the public; to the specialist perhaps only as good as the detail with which changes are recorded. It is essential to be clear about the aims and means of conservation, and to acknowledge that restoration in this century will rightly be seen by succeeding generations as another of the overlapping cycles of design. It is already possible to look back at the restoration of formal gardens at the end of the last century and see them in context, as part of an eclectic tradition. In the 1930s attempts at the re-creation of gardens in a historical manner illustrated concern with the conservation of a national cultural heritage. At Herrenhausen, when the Baroque garden was restored, this led to the creation of new 'special' gardens which emphasised the Lower German, rather than the French, influence on the development of German garden design. Other re-creations were no more historically accurate, even if less overtly nationalistic. The planting of the castle garden at Edzell is authentic neither in layout nor in detail.

26 The gardens at Villandry – a twentieth-century re-creation using designs from sixteenth-century engravings

27 One of the small gardens at Colonial Williamsburg which represents a 1930s ideal of a colonial garden

Two trenches were dug across the site, but yielded little more than an indication of some sort of central feature. It was in America that the first serious attempt to restore a garden on the basis of archaeological investigation was carried out, at Colonial Williamsburg, but, by and large, where considerations of beauty and accuracy were in conflict, beauty won, and the gardens represent a 1930s ideal of their colonial counterparts. Despite archaeological investigation at Kirby Hall in Northamptonshire, England, most of the 1690s layout was destroyed by the subsequent 'restoration', and here again the details and planting which replaced it have no authentic basis.

Much of the significance of Kirby Hall lies in the early use of archaeological investigation in a historic garden, and the lessons learnt from it. Further archaeological investigation at Kirby in the 1980s has revealed the limitations of the work done in the 1930s, uncovering more evidence of the earlier 1640s garden than that of the 1690s, and enabling English Heritage to contemplate the possibility of a much more accurate restoration, at least in part, if sufficient evidence is found. The destruction of archaeological evidence and the loss of files from the 1930s illustrate the importance of the making and safe-keeping of clear records of both the survey work and the changes made.

Public interest and education

At both Edzell and Kirby Hall the re-creation has, until recently, been presented to the public as a truthful representation of an early garden. Public concern is a necessary prerequisite to the protection of heritage gardens, but that concern will only be expressed by an informed and interested public. Interest must be stimulated at the garden gate. At Kirby the opportunity has been grasped to capture public interest, and to enhance perception of the problems involved, by good presentation of the history of the garden, its restoration, and the current archaeological investigations. At Edzell a leaflet explaining the history of the replanting of the garden in the 1930s was produced to supplement the guidebook until the information could be incorporated into a new guidebook. In contrast, the elaborate, glossy guidebook for Vaux-le-Vicomte devotes barely a paragraph to the work carried out on the gardens during the last century, and fails to attribute any part of the design of the restoration to Henri Duchêne, but claims that the work has returned the gardens to their seventeenth-century state. The work of Henri Duchêne's landscape practice, continued by his son Achille, made a vital contribution to the revival of the 'jardin à la française' around the turn of the century; to ignore it at Vaux is to ignore an important period in the development of garden design as well as to present a false picture of a seventeenth-century garden.

Accurate presentation is meaningless, however, unless visitors are first attracted to the garden, where, perhaps more than with any other art form, understanding is well-nigh impossible without first-hand experience, not only because most people find it difficult to visualise scale from photographs, plans or other documentary evidence, but also because the experience of a garden is made up of changing views and sensations, scent, sound and seasonal subtleties of colour. In Britain there is a justifiable tendency to assume that interest in gardens and garden visiting is increasing.[5] In other countries this interest may be lacking, and the first task of those involved in the conservation of gardens is to draw the visitor into the garden.

In France, despite the fact that the end of the Second World War created a climate conducive to the rise of French nationalism and a consequent heightening of interest in France's cultural heritage, the French public is largely ignorant of the wealth of French gardens. It is Versailles in its present depleted form, minus the parterres of broderie, minus the climbing plants which should transform the trellis fences into green barriers, minus the potted bedding plants which used to give colour and interest in the bosquets, with little in fact remaining of its original state except in plan, that nonetheless epitomises the French garden in the French mind. The recent promotion, for the second consecutive year, of a month of garden visiting in June 1989 by the Ministère de la Culture, in co-operation with various other organisations, has had limited impact on their perception. The free guide was not freely available except on request in the bureau of the Ministère de la Culture in 1989, and it failed to seize the opportunity to explain and promote the importance of the French contribution to the history of garden design, which, by appealing to a natural national pride, might have extended interest in gardens to a wider audience.

The history of heritage conservation in the United States has revolved around the association of places with historic events or personalities. The Americans are fortunate that two of their early presidents, George Washington and Thomas Jefferson, were both keen gardeners. This has enabled them to harness the interests of garden conservation to the maintenance of Mount Vernon and Monticello as commemorative monuments to their original owners. The work of the Thomas Jefferson Foundation at Monticello in particular, especially since the establishment of the Thomas Jefferson Center for Historic Plants in 1987, has actively encouraged interest in historic gardens and plants.

Even where garden visiting is an established leisure activity, general perceptions of the importance of gardens, their contribution to our heritage, and the need for conservation and management, are difficult to change. Formal gardens have distinct boundaries and their design form is easily recognised. They tend to suffer when hidden by a boundary wall because they are forgotten and neglected, but simply drawing attention to their existence may overcome much of the problem of neglect. Informal woodland or landscape gardens blend into nature, making it difficult to recognise their design element, or to distinguish the boundary between garden and countryside. Such gardens are more likely to suffer destruction through ignorance than from simple neglect, and the battle to alert the public to their importance is more complex. In Britain, the sheer number of gardens, the popularity of gardening as a hobby, and public antagonism to change in gardens which are much visited add to the difficulties. In West Germany a lack of understanding of the differences between natural and designed landscapes, and ignorance of how plants grow and of their need for management, have led to political opposition to conservation measures, such as the felling and replacement of trees, in historic gardens. The situation is exacerbated because many of the most significant historic gardens are now state owned and serve a dual function as both garden and public park, and, since it is easier to make political mileage out of proposed changes in a much visited garden, attention has been directed towards nature within gardens rather than in the wider countryside. In America the recent recognition of the importance of Frederick Law Olmsted as an early pioneer in the development of landscape design has focused attention on the 'preservation'[6] and restoration of Olmsted parks and gardens, and helped improve public consciousness of the distinction between natural and designed landscapes. However there is a danger that the cult of personalities in the American conservation movement may result in many, equally important, gardens by lesser or unknown mortals being overlooked.

Two of the options open to managers of individual gardens in trying to extend public interest and understanding are the use of the media, and the provision of educational programmes for schoolchildren. Regular press releases can bring welcome publicity, but their timing is important. A story anticipating the felling and replacement of an avenue, for example, can be a political disaster if released when there is already public outcry over the felling of woodland for agriculture or development, but if presented as a success story after replanting is complete, perhaps in the context of other conservation projects, its effect will be quite different. Advertising too should be carefully planned. It is always more effective if it coincides with feature articles on related subjects. The involvement of schoolchildren in garden projects not only helps broaden the understanding of a new generation, but draws the interest of parents and families also. At Painshill staff cooperated in an experimental summer school in 1989, dressing up to stage a very enjoyable treasure hunt for various eighteenth-century objects which 'Charles Hamilton' asked the participants to help him find. Ideas do not have to be elaborate to appeal to the imagination. Encouraging children to help with tree planting and to monitor the progress of the plants, holding workshops for garden-related activities or running work programmes for older children, are all ideas which have been successfully attempted. At Levens Hall in Cumbria there is a special quiz book for children, and the education departments of museums and galleries have often produced excellent information packs. But, while local publicity is important, a more comprehensive approach is needed to stimulate general public awareness of the value of conservation. In this regard the role of voluntary organisations is crucial since it is organisations, with the ability to call on a bevy of specialist expertise, which can most effectively promote education, and bring pressure to bear on governments, owners and developers.

The roles of government, national and international bodies

The history of the conservation movement in Britain demonstrates the efficacy with which voluntary organisations have influenced government action. The beginnings of the Historic Buildings and Monuments Commission (for England and Wales) and the Historic Buildings and Monuments Directorate of the Scottish Development Department[7] can be traced to the founding of the Society for the Protection of Ancient Buildings in 1877. The National Parks Commission, replaced by the Countryside Commission in 1968, was the direct result of the lobbying of government by the Society for the Promotion of Nature Reserves, together with the Royal Society for the Protection of Birds and other amenity organisations such as the Commons, Open Spaces and Footpaths Preservation Society. The campaign was taken up by the Council for the Protection of Rural England on its inception in 1926. The Countryside Commission is an advisory and promotional body with grant awarding powers. Unlike the American National Park Service, the Countryside Commission and its predecessor, the National Parks Commission, never had a landholding role, largely because of the existence of the National Trust for Places of Historic Interest or Natural Beauty. The National Trust was founded in 1895, and made a statutory body by the first National Trust Act, in 1907, which gave it power to hold land in perpetuity for the benefit of the nation. The constitution of the National Trust was based on that of the Trustees of Public Reservations, founded in Massachusetts in 1891. Both recognised the need to own and manage land in order to ensure its effective protection. In 1931 a similar trust was set up for Scotland on the initiative of the Association for the Protection of Rural Scotland, and the same power invested in it by the National Trust for Scotland Act of 1935.

The role of the National Trusts is threefold: in conservation, education and recreation. Until recently the National Trust has taken its recreational responsibilities with regard to gardens more seriously than its educational ones, treating gardens more often as a foil to a country house than as of historical significance in their own right. Early acquisitions of gardens were either the result of the Country House Scheme started in 1937, or were made more for their aesthetic and planting merits under a scheme initiated with the Royal Horticultural Society in 1948, and from the beginning the Trust has concentrated its attention on the care of its own properties and their enjoyment by its membership. The National Trust for Scotland's interpretation of its responsibilities is slightly different. It sees its main role as the promotion of the conservation, not merely of its own properties but of landscape, wildlife and buildings in Scotland in general. The resources of the Scottish Trust are limited however, and the realisation of these responsibilities has been less than evident in the field of garden conservation. It is the National Trust in England that has been widely respected for its lead in garden conservation since the early 1970s, and the Trust now has an enviable record on garden surveys, and is becoming increasingly skilled at balancing the requirements of accurate restoration with reasonable maintenance and the presentation of the garden to the visitor.

Encouragement for a greater degree of accuracy in restoration work has come from the work and research of other organisations recently formed to promote various aspects of the conservation of gardens. In 1978 the Royal Horticultural Society was the instigator of the formation of the National Council for the Conservation of Plants and Gardens. It runs a system for cataloguing plants and gardens from the RHS garden at Wisley, and has initiated the National Plant Collections, set up to try to conserve old-fashioned and rare varieties of garden plants. The Garden History Society, founded in 1965, has gradually taken over the role of national watchdog on historic parks and gardens, which was lacking in the work of the National Trust. It has earned an authoritative standing through its academic journal and the collation of research work by its members, and has been notably successful in pursuing Public Inquiries where historic parks have been under threat.[8] Similar organisations to these exist in other countries.[9]

One of the most important requirements for the successful protection of gardens is a comprehensive inventory. The assessment of the significance of a garden can only be made within an international, national or local context and in relation to others of its type. In some countries the starting of an inventory by an independent body has effectively pressured government into producing an official list of significant parks and gardens as a first step towards protection, but since any official list must inevitably be concise rather than comprehensive, inventories are an invaluable tool for the conservationist. In West Germany the Deutsche Gesellschaft für Gartenkunst und Landschaftspflege completed a preliminary private survey of historic gardens, 'Erfassung der historischen Gärten und Parks in der Bundesrepublik Deutschland', in 1980. Publication was sponsored by the heritage conservation society, Deutscher Heimatbund, and it was distributed for correction, amendment and addition. It is now into a second edition but it is by no means complete. It was intended to be a means to nudge the Bundesländer administrations to further action. Few states listed gardens as protected monuments prior to this (Niedersachsen was the first to make a start in 1981), and even where they were listed, usually only formal gardens were recognised. The fullest list is currently being compiled in Berlin where the availability of ample funds for cultural projects enabled the administration to set up a 'Gartendenkmalpflege' section under the Institute of Urban Development and Environmental Protection in 1978 with a team of qualified staff. 1984 saw the start of a seven-year programme to list both private gardens and public open spaces in a house to house survey. Such an expensive exercise is possible only in Berlin, but it gives an ideal model for others to aspire to copy.

The Garden History Society started a survey of gardens in England and Wales in 1973 and produced a 'Preliminary List of Gardens, Parks, Grounds and Designed Landscapes of Historic Interest for England and Wales' in 1976, the same year that the UK Gardens Committee of the UNESCO sponsored organisation ICOMOS (International Council on Monuments and Sites) initiated its preliminary and interim *List of Gardens and Parks of Outstanding Historic Interest* which applied to Scotland also and was published in 1979. These moves were followed by the compiling of a *Register of Parks and Gardens of Special Historic Interest* by the Historic Buildings and Monuments Commission (1984) and an *Inventory of Gardens and Designed Landscapes in Scotland*, commissioned from Land Use Consultants by the Scottish Development Department and the Countryside Commission for Scotland (1987). None of these British lists, registers or inventories can be said to be comprehensive. The task of producing a truly comprehensive inventory has fallen to the Centre for the Conservation of Historic Parks and Gardens which was established within the Institute for Advanced Architectural Studies at York University on the initiative, and with the financial support of the Countryside Commission in 1982.

The role of the York Centre extends to information exchange and research on all topics relating to garden conservation, the production of publications, the running of an education programme and consultancy. A similar remit on environmental interpretation, including the presentation of gardens, is held by the Centre for Environmental Interpretation at Manchester Polytechnic, established in 1980 with grant aid from the Carnegie United Kingdom Trust. Representatives from various agencies including the Countryside Commission, the Civic Trust, the Society for the Interpretation of Britain's Heritage, the Welsh Development Agency and the National Trust for Scotland advise on policy. These initiatives show great imagination in the application of grant aid. The Countryside Commission also administers specific grants for professional advice for the restoration and management of parks and gardens outwith urban areas. The Hampshire Gardens Trust, the first of a series of independent County Trusts in England formed with the support of the local authority to promote the interests of local gardens and to press for listed status where appropriate, employs a part-time secretary, funded by the Countryside Commission, because of the help which it in turn gives towards starting new trusts. Unlike other government agencies, the Countryside Commission's grant awarding powers for individual sites need not be conditional on giving reasonable access to the public, but it has been able to insist on the production of a comprehensive management plan for restoration as a condition of grant aid.[10] On Countryside Commission advice the Hampshire Gardens Trust also insists on a management and maintenance plan being agreed with the Trust when grant aid is given. A similar requirement for a survey report, including historic research, and a management plan is made a condition of financial help to members of the state subsidised Stichting Particuliere Historische Buitenplaatsen (Society for Private Historic Estates) in the Netherlands.

The responsibilities of owners and sources of finance

The responsibilities of owners in the face of a new understanding of the importance of conservation are arduous. Without financial assistance from government sources few of the larger historic gardens in private ownership would be able to survive in anything like their original form. The provision of capital grants is relatively simple; grants for maintenance are generally more difficult to administer. Some government help has been forthcoming in the provision of direct labour schemes such as the Youth Training Scheme in Britain where the government will pay the wage of a young trainee, or the provision of a set number of hours of labour by the SPHB to its members in the Netherlands, if the garden is opened to the public. In many countries, as in the

Netherlands, private owners have come together to form associations to assist each other and to give them a stronger voice at government level. In France the Vieilles Maisons Françaises is such a body, and in Belgium, L'Association Royale des Demeures Historiques de Belgique has been formed to promote paying visitors. The upkeep of gardens is costly and the encouragement of visitors is one of the few ways in which owners can increase revenue for garden maintenance. Where gardens attract a sufficient number of visitors it may be possible to obtain business sponsorship: plants and tools from local nurseries and manufacturers, or facilities for printing a guidebook. There are some private charitable trusts also which may give money towards repair and maintenance.[11] In Britain, besides the grants available for historic gardens from the Countryside Commission, English Heritage and, in the case of gardens attached to historic buildings, the Scottish Development Department, there are others administered by different government agencies for specific purposes. The Scottish Tourist Board is a possible source of funds if visitor numbers merit the development of tourist facilities. Grants for planting are available from the Forestry Commission under its Woodland Grant Scheme, and the Countryside Commission, the Countryside Council for Wales (a new amalgamation of the Countryside Commission and the Nature Conservancy Council which was inaugurated in April 1991) and the Countryside Commission for Scotland[12] grant aid landscape work for the improvement of gardens and estates in rural areas.

The conservation of a garden can be a daunting task in management terms, and one which many private owners are unwilling to undertake, especially when a garden has suffered years of neglect and requires major restoration for which grants from government bodies can meet only part of the expenditure. English Heritage grants, for example, usually cover a maximum of forty per cent of the total costs of any one project. For this reason the ownership and management of a garden has sometimes been taken over by a charitable trust, either through the gift of the owner who remains a trustee, or through the acquisition of the garden by a local trust. Charities in most countries incur favourable tax concessions. In Britain the National Heritage Memorial Fund, created in 1980, is able to provide money for the purchase of significant gardens under threat. It deals only with applications from local authorities or charitable trusts, and both Painshill Park and Chatelherault are examples where the capital costs of the acquisition and restoration were defrayed by the fund.

Legislation and grant aid

It is difficult to strike a balance between interference and reasonable control in legislation concerning the conservation of private properties. In countries where, historically, bureaucratic interference is resented, the problem is more acute. How far does government have the right to dictate to private owners? In the United States, where the right of owners over their own property is considered inviolate, the problem has been side-stepped, and legislation has concentrated purely on the threat to conservation from the actions of government. Government grants for important historic gardens in the private sector have been available in West Germany since 1979, but, because of the conditions imposed, few are taken up. Most legislation specifically introduced for the protection of gardens and parks has been directed towards alerting owners to their responsibilities and encouraging restoration through financial incentives. Because of the fragile nature of gardens it is difficult to formulate legislation which has sufficient bite, and the protection of gardens usually depends on the proffering of a carrot rather than the wielding of a stick, but grants from government sources are, of necessity, generally limited to gardens which are included in statutorily recognised lists or registers.

In England the National Heritage Act 1983 enabled English Heritage (the Historic Buildings and Monuments Commission) to compile an official register on a similar basis to the provisions made for listing buildings in the 1971 Town and Country Planning Act. The register now comprises 1,173 sites, and owners as well as local planning authorities and the Secretary of State must be sent a copy of the entries. Since the Town and Country Amenities Act 1974 it has been theoretically possible to give grants towards the cost of the 'upkeep of historic gardens and other land which appear to the Secretary of State to be of outstanding interest'. In practice funds have not been available, and only where gardens contained listed buildings did they attract grants, although where buildings form part of an outstanding landscape all attract grants regardless of whether all are listed. Following high winds in the south of England in October 1987, the government made money available to both English Heritage and the Countryside Commission (Task Force Trees) for grant aid to any storm damaged properties, even if not on the register. There is no comparable legislation for a register of gardens in Scotland, and storm damage in Europe's windiest country tends to occur steadily rather than in sudden devastation, but, as in England, garden buildings may be listed and eligible for grants under the Town and Country Planning (Scotland) Act 1972.

Whereas listing affords statutory protection in that official consent must be obtained before any listed structure is demolished, the register is purely advisory. In both countries further protection for gardens may be afforded by the designation of Conservation Areas under the two Town and Country Planning Acts. Such a designation is not limited to areas containing historic buildings, and the treatment of gardens can form part of a grant-aided scheme for the 'enhancement' of a Conservation Area. The only planted elements subject to actual controls, however, are trees. The local planning authority must be given six weeks' notice prior to the start of any work on trees in a Conservation Area. This enables the issue of a Tree Preservation Order which prohibits the felling, topping or lopping of trees without permission, and allows for permission to be conditional on replacement planting. Local authorities in England have additional powers to give grants for gardens under the Civic Amenities Act 1974. Hampshire County Council took advantage of this piece of legislation to support the formation of the Hampshire Gardens Trust.

The criteria for the legislative protection of parks and gardens in Britain, whether by inclusion in the register, or by designation of a Conservation Area, is 'historic' interest. In America too, historic interest is the only criterion for nomination to the National Register of Historic Places. The danger in the use of historic interest only, to justify protection, is that more importance may be given to the association of a garden with historic events or personalities than to the aesthetic or cultural value of the garden itself. English Heritage is trying to address this problem by devising guidelines, primarily for the care and restoration of its own garden properties, but also to be taken into account when considering grant applications or giving advice, and the National Park Service has produced a technical bulletin (National Register Bulletin 18) on 'How to evaluate and nominate designed historic landscapes'. In Italy a statute passed in 1939 extended the protection of villas, parks and gardens to those of artistic and historic interest. The Italian Charter[13] also defines gardens more broadly than in the ICOMOS Charter of Florence by extending the definition to include green spaces in historic town centres. The Istituto Centrale per il Catalogo e la Documentazione, the technical and scientific arm of the Ministero per i Beni Culturali e Ambientali, has researched a method for compiling inventories of gardens covered in the 1939 statute. Each region is responsible for the conservation of gardens within its boundaries. The approach taken therefore differs, and the inventories are in varying stages of completion. In the former West Germany also, measures for the protection of gardens differ from state to state as each state is independent on cultural matters, but from 1971 to 1980 gardens were included in statutes for the protection of historic monuments. Gardens are usually covered by the Ministry of Culture, but in some states, for example Bayern, they are under the

Ministry of Finance, and in a few there is as yet no specific provision. Where they are listed they will eventually be included in the published volumes of *Denkmaltopographie Bundesrepublik Deutschland* which are well illustrated with photographs and available to the public in bookshops. Some 538 gardens are classified as historic monuments in France under the care of the Ministère de la Culture. In addition, in 1983 the Decentralisation Act provided for the establishment of Zones of Architectural and Urban Heritage Protection (ZAPPU) to be administered by the regional office of the Ministère de l'Equipement. Gardens are included as ZAPPU but as yet the inventory is incomplete.

The conservation process

2

Assessment and evaluation

An assessment of the value and potential of a garden is a vital first step in deciding what approach should be taken towards conservation. Resources are limited, particularly for those gardens which can be statutorily protected, and so it is necessary to determine criteria by which to judge a garden's significance. The assessment of a garden must be based on an understanding of its present nature, its history and its relationship to other gardens of a comparable type. The usefulness of any inventory of gardens depends on how comprehensive it is, how consistent in its assessment of gardens, and the method of recording. These factors are crucial to the determination of the importance of a garden in the context of others.

Since in many countries gardens are protected as historic monuments, and since too legislation for the protection of gardens has followed that for buildings, the assessment of a garden has usually depended first, and sometimes solely, on its historic interest. Although historic interest is generally fairly widely interpreted, a garden is primarily a pleasure ground. Its architectural features, structural elements such as hedges and trees, and its planting design, all contribute to beauty and enjoyment, and its interest and value may be enhanced by horticultural, arboricultural or sylvicultural interest, or by scenic and ecological qualities. The consideration of a garden's contribution to our heritage should not have to wait until it can be classed as 'historic'. One only has to look at the sad state of disrepair of Monet's garden at Giverny when its rescue began in 1977 to see what can happen in the fifty years or so that it takes to recognise a garden as historic (Monet died in 1926), especially when plants and plant combinations determine the garden's character. Yet Monet's garden is a prime example of one which, even in the painter's lifetime, was significant for its aesthetic qualities, as a horticultural work of art where plants replaced paints on a canvas of earth. It would be sad indeed if every garden had to wait to become 'historic' before being given the benefit of protection. Nevertheless, during the ownership of its creator a garden is a changing, evolving and dynamic work which must in some sense be completed before conservation is appropriate. In practice therefore, the evaluation of a garden for conservation purposes is rarely an issue before the death of the original owner or designer.

ARTISTIC VALUE

A garden is a designed landscape, and one that is designed first and foremost for enjoyment. As such it should be assessed in artistic as well as historical and cultural terms. Its assessment should consider the integrity of the design as it exists today, and whether it still reflects the original intentions of the designer. Its artistic value will depend on whether it remains true to its conception as a work of art more than on a subjective assessment of beauty which is liable to change as tastes change. Some weight should be given however to its scenic qualities, the views, design form and plantings as they contribute to the enjoyment of the users of today.

HISTORICAL VALUE

Historical value may be ascribed to a garden for various reasons. A garden may be an exceptional example in representing the taste or style of any one period, such as the late seventeenth century, Dutch style, formal canal garden at Westbury Court. It may demonstrate a continuous history where the complex overlay of features from different periods illustrates changing fashions and the evolutionary process of gardening and garden design, for instance in the redesign of a formal garden near the house in the late eighteenth or early nineteenth century to reverse the ravages of the landscape garden, or, as at Crathes Castle in Aberdeenshire, Scotland, in the design of herbaceous and shrub borders early this century, using new plant introductions, within the structure of the old walled garden. The association of a garden with a historic personality can also contribute to historic value, although one should be wary of placing too much emphasis on this criterion if the present layout of the garden no longer retains a reasonable number of features from the same period. In their guidelines for the evaluation of historic landscape according to National Register criteria the American National Park Service are at pains to point out that where a designed landscape assumes value because of its association with a historic figure that person should have been significantly involved in landscape architecture, gardening or planning.

CULTURAL VALUE

The judgement of the degree of significance of a garden will vary according to the context in which it is assessed, whether local, regional, national or international. Westbury Court is a rare example of a Dutch canal garden of which few survive even in the Netherlands, and it therefore assumes significance in an international context, Vaux-le-Vicomte represents the peak of achievement in French garden art of its period and is therefore outstanding on a national scale. But because of the influence of Le Notre, the later restoration work of the Duchênes and in turn their contribution to the return of the formal garden 'à la française' elsewhere at the end of the nineteenth century, it is also outstanding on an international scale. A garden may be of a type comparable to many others on a national level, but significant locally where it is the only example of its type, or because it includes the work of local craftsmen. The cultural value of a garden in relation to the gardening traditions of its geographical locality, whether national or local, is something that is often overlooked. Where an assessment is attempted without a general understanding of the background of prevailing traditions and garden history, it can result in misleading judgements of a garden's significance. Land Use Consultants betrayed some of this confusion in their recent Scottish inventory when, for example, they prefaced their comments on Pluscarden Abbey by pointing out that there is no large designed landscape attached to it. In a Scottish context a large designed landscape attached to a twelfth-century abbey would indeed be surprising; in an English context perhaps less so. A Scottish inventory however should pertain to Scotland and to Scottish cultural traditions, and those making assessments should beware neighbouring influences on their judgement.

CHECKLISTS AND SURVEYS

When making an initial assessment of the merits of an individual garden as a prelude to a conservation project it is helpful to use a checklist. The Survey and Inventory Site Recommendation and Site Report forms and guidance notes, available from the Centre for the Conservation of Historic Parks and Gardens, Institute of Advanced Architectural Studies, University of York, are a useful tool, and a uniform approach facilitates comparisons with other gardens. Similar forms, such as the American National Register of Historic Places Registration Form, are available in other countries. Any assessment has an element of subjective judgement and it is therefore wise to carry out a fresh assessment even when an inventory entry already exists. A knowledge of other gardens in the geographic area, and of other gardens of the same type is essential when making value judgements, and visits should be arranged to draw comparisons. The particular merits of the garden can then be summarised within various categories: its quality and integrity as a work of art; historic interest; cultural interest; architectural qualities; scenic qualities; botanical and ecological interest. A survey carried out for the evaluation of a garden will be done in less depth than one on which a detailed conservation and maintenance plan is based, but from such a study and assessment it should be possible to determine the broad outline of an appropriate conservation policy.

Conservation policy

CONSERVATION

The conservation of gardens is the deliberate, planned and thoughtful treatment of gardens, managed to balance their protection and upkeep with the realisation of their full potential for enjoyment and education. The value and attraction of any one garden depends on the approach taken towards its conservation, and the method chosen will depend on its type and size, its state of repair, the availability of historical information, its potential as a recreational or educational resource and how it is to be used. Some degree of restoration, whether full or partial reinstatement of an original design from an earlier period or periods, or repair or renewal of some features of the garden, or just improvement to the general condition of the garden, will usually be necessary, but a 'conserve as found' policy is increasingly being advocated.

PRESERVATION

In garden terms a strict 'conserve as found', or preservation, policy is rarely appropriate because of the ephemerality of the principal medium, the plants. Where a garden exists only as a monument and is no longer actively used, preservation is possible. One example is the King's Knot, Stirling, where the form of the garden is still visible in the contours of the ground, which is now grassed over. The garden is preserved from further decay by simple maintenance of the greensward. To 'conserve as found' in a garden still in active use involves sympathetic care and maintenance, but if planted elements are not renewed its character will gradually be eroded. This may be acceptable where a garden's main features are architectural or where restoration measures would threaten the garden's value as a historical document. It may even be acceptable for a limited number of years until major planted elements such as avenues are no longer viable, but in general some renewal or repair is essential in a creative conservation programme.

RESTORATION

Restoration, the attempt to return a garden to its original form or forms and to a viable state of upkeep within a normal maintenance routine, is usually the preferred means of conservation where a garden has suffered from neglect or from changes due to inadequate management or lack of resources. The standard of historical restoration often leaves a lot to be desired. The reasons are many and various. First, there is often a lack of historical documentation and evidence. Second, information obtained from historical research and survey work is subject to mistakes and misinterpretation. Third, field survey work, although an essential tool, usually gives only approximate clues to historical fact, and the correlation and interpretation of information require imaginative guess-work backed by persistent cross-checking. Fourth, our technical knowledge pertaining to the re-creation of authentic detail is limited, particularly in planting design. Fifth, historical interests have to be balanced with others – horticultural, artistic, recreational, educational and ecological – and this balancing act is often short-sighted in its policy and implementation. Finally, all these problems are compounded by inadequate resources of labour and finance, and in view of the difficulties involved, it is wise to proceed with caution, essential to keep clear records, and desirable, as far as possible, to make restoration measures reversible where there is any doubt as to their accuracy.

The most straightforward form of restoration is the repair of structural fabric, and renewal of planting. Where simple repairs can be made, authentic details and materials should be used and matched to the original fabric. Where details cannot be matched because of the loss of original fabric and lack of historical information, the repair should be clearly recorded. Sometimes a repair can be delineated without detriment to the overall appearance so that there is no mistaking new fabric for the original. In the rebuilding of the boundary wall to the Charles Carroll garden, Annapolis, for example, the old brick surface stands proud of the new. Where planting needs attention the issues are always complicated. The cost of maintenance, for instance of nineteenth-century bedding schemes, can be prohibitive and lead to a decision to restore only the basic form of the garden without replanting herbaceous or smaller shrub material. Usually such a decision is reversible but the importance of accurate recording with planting plans and photographs both before and after restoration, to allow the decision to be reviewed in future, cannot be over-emphasised.

The treatment of avenues is a good example of the difficulties which must be faced in deciding to what degree the replanting of the more permanent features is appropriate. The form of an avenue depends for its effect on the straight, parallel lines of regularly spaced and even-aged trunks. When trees die or otherwise need replacement, there are various alternatives to consider. The first alternative is to leave the gaps in the line until all the trees have to be felled, in order to preserve the actual historic component as long as possible. A toothless hag has character but lacks the beauty of youth. The second alternative therefore is to replant the gaps, but in this case the regular appearance of trees of the same age will be lost. The third alternative is to replant on either side of the existing avenue, and fell the old trees when the new avenue is sufficiently mature, but the loss of both the historic line and the proportions of the avenue will result. The fourth alternative is simply to clear fell and replant. Except where the trees have been subject to disease, it is usually feasible to use the same species, or even to propagate from the existing stock so that in time the effect will be as near that of the original conception as possible. The decision rests on whether it is more important to try to retain the garden's artistic or historic integrity and each case will depend on its merits.

The restoration of a garden may be compromised for reasons other than the nature of the plant material or the limitations on research and available historical information. Few heritage gardens remain completely private; most have to adapt to an influx of visitors as they open to the public. This may lead to a policy decision to use different materials to reduce wear and tear, or to alterations to reduce the visual impact of large numbers of visitors. In other gardens the loss of one feature, which it is not practical to replace, may alter the balance of the design so that changes to the layout are deemed more in keeping with the spirit of the original. At Giverny the main paths used by visitors have been resurfaced with concrete instead of gravel, but using the same gravel aggregate so that the visual intrusion is minimised. At Stourhead the path has been moved away from the lake and up into the wood, both to counter erosion of the lakeside and to hide visitors from each other, so that the peace and tranquillity of the eighteenth-century vision remains intact.

The conservation process

28 Clarity of execution – the repair to the boundary wall of the Charles Carroll garden

29 A complete reconstruction – the William Paca garden, Annapolis

Heritage Gardens

RE-CREATION

In the examples described above, the restoration has been consciously modified. Modifications should always be clearly recorded, not only for future use by professionals involved in restoration and upkeep, but also as interpretative information available to the public, so that changes are not passed off as part of the original design. When well presented, the reasons behind particular restoration decisions and information on the process of restoration itself add considerably to the interest of the garden as a whole, and aid the imaginative interpretation of what the garden once was. In its most extreme form a modified restoration is sometimes termed a 'restoration-in-spirit'. The use of the term 'restoration' is scarcely justified here because the primary objective is not accuracy, but rather an attempt to reinterpret the original intentions of the designer. This is of dubious value in conservation terms, and is closer in concept to a re-creation. The garden at Edzell Castle is a re-creation which attempts to express something of the spirit of an early seventeenth-century garden. At Pitmedden the re-creation purports to be a more accurate representation of a seventeenth-century garden, and as such is a 'period garden' re-created on an existing site. The dividing line is thin, and, even when its origins are well presented, the re-creation of a garden, particularly a period garden, on an existing site can be misleading. A period garden should properly be seen as one means of explaining to the public the features of a garden of a particular historic period. They are liable to become 'heritage gardens' only in terms of the perception of future generations or their intrinsic artistic merit, if at all, and their creation on a genuine historic site can only be confusing.

RECONSTRUCTION

Where a garden has been completely, or almost completely, destroyed but is both judged to be of great significance and sufficiently well-recorded, restoration may take the form of a reconstruction. A reconstruction differs from a re-creation in its attempt to be a historically accurate re-modelling of a garden which was known to exist on the site. The recent development of new techniques of archaeological investigation has facilitated reconstructions where previously they would have proved impossible. The William Paca garden in Annapolis, Maryland, has been reconstructed in just such a manner, from archaeological evidence and little else. Before restoration the garden was buried under a hotel and three metres of fill. It is inevitable, in a complete reconstruction of this type, that the detail will not replicate the original garden exactly, unless there is a wealth of documentary evidence. How gratifying, therefore, when a clump of bulrushes appeared in the 'eye' of the reconstructed fish-shaped pond! It is often planting details which are the most difficult to reproduce. Other details can at least be copied from known examples authentic to the period.

At Het Loo however it is the planting which has been painstakingly researched and copied, while the construction details are an unashamed deception, re-creating the appearance of a historic garden by using modern construction techniques and materials under the surface. This reconstruction is unarguably modern, but has been justified in terms of its setting for the palace as a museum and the numbers of visitors it has already attracted.

POLICY DECISIONS

Wherever reconstruction, re-creation or a modified restoration are implemented the destruction of archaeological and field evidence is the inevitable result. Careful consideration must therefore be given to the importance of the site as a recreational, educational or archaeological resource, and whether the loss of source material can be justified by the gains to be had from the treatment proposed. Where much of the garden still exists above ground and less drastic action is needed to restore it to, or close to, its original form, hesitation can result in further loss. Where most of the evidence is below ground, the situation is reversed and, if it is not possible to make provision for a very detailed investigation and recording of the site before undertaking restoration on a major scale, conservation of the site as it stands is preferable.

Design and presentation

Design objectives need to be just as clearly formulated for conservation as for a new design project. How a garden should be conserved and managed depends just as much on its use, the numbers of visitors it is likely to attract, as on its historic, cultural or artistic significance. Costs must be carefully balanced against capital and projected income figures, and the method of restoration decided in the light of the labour available, whether regular garden staff or outside contractors. Following the initial assessment of the garden it should be possible to write a broad policy statement, describing to which period or periods the garden should be restored, which are its most significant features, the principles on which they should be maintained, and the management of visitors. An example of a policy statement of this sort is that devised for the Hercules Garden, Blair Castle (see below, p. 162). A statement of the design objectives will clarify the need for further site investigation and the form it should take, and detailed design proposals and a maintenance plan can then be worked out within the stated guidelines.

It is important to realise that good presentation and interpretation of the particular significance of a garden can be a useful tool at every stage of the restoration process to people involved on every level, and not merely to the public when the garden is finally opened. A clear statement of objectives and the reasons behind them can become an early part of the interpretative process, encouraging co-operation between professionals and owners. In the case of the proposed restoration at Hawkstone, Shropshire, a well produced leaflet outlining the history and importance of the site, the broad aims for conservation and proposals for co-operation was distributed to seek support prior to the setting up of a Trust to manage the rescue operation.

METHODS OF PRESENTATION

It is as well to consider methods of presentation and interpretative education when formulating the design objectives. Interest in a garden can be generated early on. The process of restoration is interesting in itself, and many of the techniques, particularly in the archaeological field, are new. The various stages of the transformation of a garden from dereliction to rebirth can often be made into a fascinating supporting exhibition through plans and photographs, and are all part of the history of the garden. Different approaches to education may be appropriate at different stages of a conservation project, and a variety of means is available to aid presentation. There are historic precedents for garden guides and guidebooks, but the use of complementary exhibition material, cassette recorders for self-guided tours, and video presentations, are modern, and their comparative advantages and disadvantages have to be carefully considered.

The **guided tour** can be particularly informative and interesting during the process of restoration when there is no 'finished' garden to enjoy, and often results in an increase in local support and frequent return visits by those eager to see how work progresses. The National Trust has received a very positive response to the introduction of guided visits during the restoration of Biddulph Grange. When the garden is fully open it is planned to employ staff in the dual role of custodian and guide in the different garden areas, much as they are employed in the rooms of National Trust houses at present. Guides can bring out different aspects of the garden in response to the interests of different groups, but a very thorough knowledge of the garden is necessary.

30 Bill Tomlins, knowledge and enthusiasm in action, leads a guided tour at Painshill

31 Life-size models of the gardener's boys in the permanent interpretative exhibition at Chatelherault

Questions can be searching and the lack of an adequate answer frustrating.

Video tapes have successfully been used to explain the restoration of the garden at Painshill Park, and to present the archaeological investigations at Kirby Hall. Since a video can be distributed and shown to a wider audience than just those visiting the garden, it can be a useful part of a more extensive publicity and education programme.

Self-guided tours by means of audio cassettes have a limited appeal in comparison to guides and guidebooks. They do not contain the visual information that can be included in a guidebook, nor the flexibility of a personal guide, and unless very well conceived can be difficult to follow. Nevertheless, as they can be switched on and off, they allow an individual to tour the garden at his own pace, and can be a good supplement to a plan and guidebook where resources do not permit the employment of guides.

Where space permits, the mounting of an **exhibition** to explain the history and upkeep of a garden can add considerably to its interest. An exhibition can include three dimensional models, sound and smell to invoke an atmosphere and stimulate the imagination, as well as historical documents, plans, pictures and photographs, and garden implements. Pots of hyacinths with their heady scent lent an evocative spirit to the exhibition on 'The Anglo-Dutch Garden in the Age of William and Mary' in the otherwise dry atmosphere of Christie's auction rooms, London, in January 1989. The permanent exhibition at Chatelherault uses life-size models to tell the story of the history of the grounds through the eyes of the huntsman, forester, stonemason and gardener. Any interpretative material has a limited life, and needs regular revision. The production of videos or expensive exhibition material of this sort can only be justified if visitor numbers are sufficient to guarantee cost effectiveness.

For all gardens open to the public, even the smallest, the production of a **guidebook** is a wise expenditure and one which can usually be recouped from sales. Even in its simplest form, a leaflet with a plan of the garden and some basic information on the main features, a printed guide is very effective. A full colour guide is often popular as a souvenir, and can be used to present more detailed information, to be perused at leisure. The leaflet and guide for the garden at Painswick are good examples. Plant lists are sometimes produced to supplement the guidebook. These can be linked to a plan or to discreet numbering which relieves the necessity for prominent labelling. Labelling can add considerably to a garden's interest but it is difficult to do effectively without visual intrusion. Materials and lettering have to be carefully chosen to be in keeping as far as possible with the general appearance of the garden.

Both the production of a guidebook and decisions on how to identify plants are considerations for the final presentation of the garden. The extent to which interest and enjoyment can be enhanced by the presentation of information still needs to be fully appreciated. The tendency to a narrow concentration on the presentation of the end result, the garden itself, ignores the benefits to be had in appealing to the visitors' imagination and leads to a presumption that aesthetic appeal is the only consideration of importance. It is all too easy to be influenced by modern tastes and fashion if aesthetic considerations are allowed to dominate. Gardens under the same ownership, for instance that of the National Trusts, can lose their individual identity in the heedless projection of a corporate image unless strenuous efforts are made to retain and enhance the individual merits of each.

PLANTING DESIGN

It is planting design which most often suffers a creeping tendency towards uniformity. Examples of modern gardens and planting proliferate; a heritage garden should present a different face to the visitor. Many a restoration scheme or garden which tries to be authentic to a certain period is marred by its planting design, even where plants of the correct period are used, and yet there are tremendous opportunities for the imaginative presentation of good, authentic planting. At Het Loo the plants are carefully spaced eighteen inches apart, a separation typical of the Dutch Baroque garden. To observe a Dutch front garden today is to observe a continuation of the same tradition. Even where bulbs are planted in groups of ten or a dozen, each is treated as a separate plant with enough space between to display it to the full height and width of its perfection. Such observations can make all the difference to the perception of planting as an interesting feature of a garden even where, from an aesthetic point of view, it seems dull. Very often, however, and particularly in the planting of parterres, accurate historic planting is very much more interesting than the common practice of using bedding plants of one colour sitting flat within box hedges, rather like a green version of a jam tart.

Pitmedden is a prime example where the planting in the parterres has all the blandness of parks department bedding dating from the nineteenth century. Judging by the numbers of visitors (25,702 in 1990 compared with 111,383 to nearby Crathes), the National Trust for Scotland is deceiving itself in claiming the use of annuals 'important to the majority of visitors who might otherwise find it difficult to experience the feeling of amazement, surprise and delight which the original garden sought to evoke'. How much more interesting it would be, and how much more appropriate to Aberdeenshire's harsh climate, as well as historically, if the plantings followed the advice of John Reid, 1683,

> For the orderly planting of flowers there may be three wayes, as first in the Bordures of Pleasure Gardens or Courts, plant 5 rowes in the bordure and Intermixe them orderly i.e. divide and plant every sundry sort through the whole garden at equal distances, and not only so but every sundry colour thereof also; let never two of a kind nor two of a colour stand together, without other kinds and colours Interveening, so as there may not be two, three of a kind or colour at one end, Bordure, Plot or Place, and non thereof through the rest, but universally and ornamentally Intermixt, and when you find a breach by some being past the flower, you may have various Annual Flowers sowen in potts, ready to plunge into the vacancies of the Bordures for continuing this beauty.

> Secondly, in my sort of flower Gardens which is Bordures and pathes running all one way viz; from the House, Plant 5 rowes and intermix them, not as in the last way, but set 5 rowes of each kind cross the Bordure, so as 25 of each sort may stand in a geometrical squair. As if you set a squair of Tulips, a squair of Boarsears a squair of Crocusues, a squair of July flowers, a squair of Anemonies, and a squair of Couslips : and so a squair of Tulips, another of Boars Ears, &c : Through that Bordure Intermixing the colours of each sort, then you may make the next Bordure so Intermixt, but differing: minding that as you Intermix the Bulbous and the Fibrous in each Bordure, so must they be also in the crossing, that the squair of Fibrous in this may oppose the squair of Bulbous in the next, and likewayes whatever Bordure such sorts ar in, on the one side of the walke, set the very same in the Bordure equidistant from the walke on the other side, that the whole may be Regular and uniformly Intermixt all the year, looking from all sides, ends or Angles.

> Thridly in nurseries of Beds and Ridges, Plant every kind in thickets by themselves, and Annualls and Perennialls by themselves (except only that you Intermix their Coloures) that is, make a whole Bed or Ridg of each kind, 6 Rowes in the Bed, the Dwarfish may be 8 Rowes : thus every thicket of them Flowering in their own order will have a great shew, and at a great distance; and here also observe uniformity, that is, alike on each hand, ... For if you have a Ridg

32 Pitmedden – bland, flat planting within the parterres

33 Herrenhausen – a pleasing experimental mixed spring planting even without the wallflowers

or Bed of *July-flowers* or the like on the one side, Plant another thereof at the same place on the other, &c.

From the description in the first paragraph it can be seen that the flowers in the parterres at Pitmedden should be an exciting mix of kind and colour. Bedding out was probably done three times a year for spring, summer and winter, but even with two plantings the season could be extended by the use of perennials. If the type of border described in the second paragraph were planted along the east, south and west walls it would obviate the need for the twentieth-century herbaceous borders planted there at present to add horticultural interest. Instead of devoting the north-east pavilion to exhibitions quite unrelated to the garden, it could then be used for a display explaining the planting of the garden and what is known of seventeenth-century planting in Scotland, and comparing the garden to others which its founder, Sir Alexander Seton, would have known, and in particular to Yester House since it is well documented in the paintings by de Witt. By these means Pitmedden could become a national showpiece, drawing visitors from all over the world.

Considerable work has been done in West Germany to develop mixed plantings for the plates-bandes which border eighteenth-century parterres. Dézallier d'Argenville's work, *La Théorie et la Pratique du Jardinage*, 1760 edition, formed the basis for the mixed plantings now carried out at Schwetzingen. The first mixed summer planting was introduced at Herrenhausen in 1988, and it is hoped that a suitable mixture for spring planting will be developed in five to six years' time. For maintenance reasons the Germans are trying to use plants which are disease resistant and unappetising. Rabbits made a meal of the wallflowers in the 1988 experimental mixed spring planting at Herrenhausen, so the quest for a good mix is not an easy one, and although the Germans use species true to the period, they are not above opting for modern varieties where they are stronger or otherwise more suitable to a modern maintenance regime. Perhaps this will become less necessary as the 'cleaning' of older varieties becomes possible.

PLANTING AND PRESENTATION

At Het Loo it is refreshing to see wall-trained fruit trees tied to the trellis with strips of willow. So often the careful selection of fruit tree varieties, painstakingly labelled with their date of introduction, is spoilt in a seventeenth- or eighteenth-century garden by heedless training on wires. The method of training on wires was not introduced until the nineteenth century and did not become common practice until the 1860s.

It is described in the 1835 edition of *An Encyclopaedia of Gardening* by J. C. Loudon:

> Some gardeners instead of using nails, drive an iron stud into all the horizontal joints of the brickwork, at the distance of 10 feet from one another, with the hole in the stud standing out half an inch from the face of the wall. Through these holes copper wires are tightly stretched from one end of the wall to another, and to this wire the branches are tied with shreds of matting.

At both Westbury Court and Pitmedden the fruit trees are trained on wires. It is hardly a mistake that can be justified on maintenance grounds since using an authentic method of training would be no more labour intensive. At Pitmedden the fruit trees on the east wall have now been moved so the opportunity presents itself to replace them with trees trained, more appropriately, by tying to nails.

Research on the planting of shrubberies in eighteenth-century gardens has been done by Mark Laird at the IASS, York, and he had put his knowledge into practice with designs for the restoration of planting at Painshill Park, Surrey. Monticello is one example of a garden where the planting was so well documented that, after meticulous research, the vegetable and flower gardens and the orchard were replanted in a true semblance of their form in the heyday of Jefferson's ownership. Garden tours have recently been introduced to complement those round the house, but when curtailed by bad weather they are liable to seem somewhat superficial. The excellent leaflets though, just designed for the vegetable and flower gardens, show how information can be both inexpensively and well presented, and will add greatly to the ready assimilation of the garden's interest. Where planting has idiosyncratic features as in Jefferson's experimental efforts at Monticello, or is a rare or unique example of accurate historic planting, as at Painshill, it is particularly important that its presentation is supplemented by good interpretative information. Both the video on the planting and the knowledge and tangible enthusiasm of the guides at Painshill are examples to emulate.

PLANTING RESEARCH

Much more research on planting design remains to be done, but the foregoing examples serve to illustrate what might be achieved if all aspects of the design and presentation of a garden are carefully considered. Where research is limited, indications for suitable types of planting can often be gleaned from practical gardening books of the relevant period, if the likely time variation between publication and practice is borne in mind. The earlier the book, the more likely it is to record established gardening practice. Thus the planting described by John Reid in 1683 can be taken as a sound basis for the planting of a garden founded in 1675 as in the case of Pitmedden. As the eighteenth century advanced, and with it interest in gardening as a fashionable pastime, the standard works of well-known garden writers tended not merely to record, but to influence gardening practice, and to introduce new ideas and methods of planting. Thus Batty Langley's *New Principles of Gardening* of 1728 was used by Washington at Mount Vernon when he started planting the pleasure grounds in 1785. By the end of the nineteenth century, writers were waxing lyrical about new ideas, and changes in fashion and practice took place much more rapidly.

Research on plant species and varieties and their dates of introduction has been more extensive than that on planting design, and in general knowledge of the history of the plants themselves is more readily available. Early herbals such as the one by Gerard give descriptive lists of cultivated plants. The book *Scotia Illustrata* by Robert Sibbald gives a complete list of garden plants grown in Scotland in the seventeenth century. John Harvey, amongst others, has compiled lists of the plants available from British nurseries at the end of the eighteenth century, and the research done by Peter Hatch at Monticello has contributed considerably to knowledge of the fruit varieties grown in America in the eighteenth century. The dates of plant introductions from the nineteenth century onwards are well recorded, and one can assume a time lag of between ten and fifteen years from the date of introduction to the date when a plant was generally available.

AUTHENTICITY IN PLANTING DESIGN

Despite the accessibility of information there has been a certain complacency in the attitude of garden conservationists towards planting. Problems of maintenance and plant availability are often given as reasons for substituting species from later periods for those known to be in use at the date a garden was planted. At Stourhead the National Trust has substituted one species of laurel, a later introduction, for the one authentic to the period because the latter grows so fast that it requires clipping. Aesthetically, however, this is not a satisfactory solution, the two species being of very different habit and growth form – it would have been better to have substituted a different genus of evergreen, but one appropriate to the period. Attitudes are changing as public interest in the history of plants, particularly those which have been in cultivation for a very long time, is increasing. The function of

34   Authentic and effective historic detail – strips of willow tie the fruit trees at Het Loo

35   Metal strip edging to a gravel path at Biltmore – modern, ugly and ineffective

heritage gardens as an educational resource should encourage owners and managers to take the initiative to ensure a greater degree of historic authenticity in their planting schemes.

PLANT AVAILABILITY

Herbaceous plantings can pose greater problems in using varieties of the correct period, especially in relation to large scale plantings such as those at Schwetzingen and Herrenhausen. A number of specialist nurseries are now making old fashioned varieties of plants more widely available and the annual publication of *The Plant Finder* by the Hardy Plant Society is of invaluable assistance in locating them. Organisations like the National Council for the Conservation of Plants and Gardens in Britain, the Hortus Bulborum in Noord-Holland and the Seed Savers Exchange in America have contributed greatly to the conservation of different plants and can help to find sources of supply. Where large numbers of plants are required though, availability can still be a problem. If space permits a plant nursery can sometimes be set up to supply a restoration project, or a local nursery might be persuaded to grow plants to order. Raising one's own plants can be unusually hazardous. At Monticello a first attempt to propagate the tennis-ball lettuce, from seeds obtained with some difficulty, came to an abrupt halt when word spread that the director thought it very tasty. Garden staff promptly polished off the rest of the lettuces, leaving none to go to seed for the following year. Often older varieties of plants are to be found in countries which were by-passed by the nineteenth-century mania for new introductions and hybrids. 'Roses du Temps Passé', an English nursery specialising in old-fashioned roses, has reintroduced many of the roses on its list from France. When propagating plants one should beware their provenance. Precious seed or stock can be wasted if grown in quite different climatic conditions from those of their place of origin unless extra care is taken to avoid losses.

DETAIL DESIGN AND THE USE OF MATERIALS

Complacency in substituting modern materials for historically accurate ones is not confined only to planting. Hard landscape also suffers from the thoughtless introduction of modern design. Edging details in particular can mar the appearance of a restoration project. New edging is frequently introduced for ease of maintenance, but it is important to assess the likely visual intrusion first. Metal strip edging is often used for gravel paths. Theoretically unobtrusive, merely a thin strip between grass and gravel, the result is often worse in practice as the gravel gets kicked away from the edge, exposing the vertical surface, or the strip has to be curved to accommodate drains. Original details should be used where possible. In respect of paths and edgings little general research has been done, but site-specific research is usually rewarding. Otherwise examples of traditional local techniques can be copied, preferably using specialist craftsmen.

There are cases where the replacement of features using substitute materials is unavoidable. At Het Loo artificial stone had to be used for the features originally made in sandstone because Dutch law forbids the carving of sandstone. Where architectural details are missing it is sometimes possible to salvage items from other sites. Seven of the stones of the central fountain at Pitmedden came from the fountain at Linlithgow cross, and it is thought that they were in fact cut by the same craftsmen as the three remaining stones from Pitmedden. Several firms now specialise in architectural salvage, and since interest in garden antiques has become so widespread there is also a growing supply of good reproductions.

Even where details are obviously not part of the original garden, but are necessary modern aids to garden management, such as information signs or barriers to keep visitors from certain areas, it is important that they are designed in a manner sympathetic to their surroundings. The green and white plastic chains used at Giverny to seal off some of the paths strike an unnecessarily discordant note against the gravel paths and vegetation. It would have been much better to have chosen a natural material. Signs and litter bins need to be not only well designed, but also carefully positioned. There is some evidence to suggest that providing litter bins actually encourages littering, and in smaller gardens it is best to confine them to the entrance, exit and car park.

DONATIONS

Donors can present problems, especially if the gift proposed is to be of a commemorative nature. Difficult to refuse, donations in kind are often accepted all too readily, even when they intrude on the design of a restoration project. The new bench at Kellie Castle is out of scale with the rest of the garden and, despite the attempt to design a piece appropriate to the turn of the century when the Lorimers revived the garden, it is out of keeping with the original concept of the garden. It is advisable to anticipate donations and to plan ahead so that suitable suggestions can be made to intending donors, or deliberately to plan to fund some features by an appeal for donations. Here again the use of a simple interpretative leaflet about the restoration can be a useful aid to channel gifts where they would be most welcome.

Costs can be prohibitive when considering the restoration of larger architectural features, glasshouses for example, expensive not only to restore but also to run. Ingenious substitutes, such as tent structures, are sometimes proposed to show the form of vanished garden buildings where they are deemed too costly to reconstruct. Especially where the foundations are still visible, an empty site has a greater romance and a more immediate appeal to the imagination when left to itself, particularly if photographs or drawings can be used as supportive information to show what was there before. On the Moseley estate, now the Maudsley State Park, in Massachusetts the foundations of the main house, with the circle terminating the entrance drive designed by Martha Brookes Hutcheson in 1906, are still clear on the ground. Standing where the house once did, it is possible to appreciate the choice of site, commanding a view of the Merrimack River, perhaps more clearly than if the house still stood.

Project organisation

The general principles for the conservation of gardens can only be translated into design practice on the basis of painstaking research, detailed survey work, long-term management plans and dedicated upkeep. The organisation of a conservation project requires the clear co-ordination of information at each stage in the conservation process to enable constant cross-checking and revision. Any project should start with the site where the main clues to a garden's form are to be found, above, on or under ground. Walking the site to note its main features, orientation, views, topography, condition and vegetation, and taking photographs and sketches in order to become familiar with the 'feel' of the landscape should be the first step before embarking on paper research to determine a garden's history.

Research

Documentary research may relate directly to the site, or to the general design and cultivation practices of the period. The latter usually becomes relevant to the project only after the design objectives are established and the motivative date for the restoration determined. Plans, maps, letters, accounts, pictures, photographs and personal recollections can all provide clues to a garden's history. Estate plans have often been discovered lying forgotten in an attic, but where there is no store of family or estate records, research should begin at the district or national records office.

Care must be taken when interpreting research information. Where early plans do exist it may be difficult to distinguish between survey plans, mapping an existing layout, and design drawings, showing new proposals which may or may not have been put into effect, although the field survey and archeological investigation can aid interpretation. Where a garden in Britain dates from before 1851 reference to the first edition of the Ordnance Survey maps, which depicted features both accurately and in detail, can be useful if subsequent changes in layout are not too drastic. Estate maps can confuse by using unfamiliar cartographic conventions. Where paintings are used for historical reference artistic licence is too often assumed; the foreground may be adapted to frame the view, but otherwise paintings are frequently surprisingly accurate. Information gained from accounts, notebooks and other papers can only be interpreted correctly if their scope and purpose are fully understood. Letters may contain private jokes or phrases no longer in common use, or be mis-read because of a lack of clarity in the handwriting. When using prints or books for research it is important to verify the date of the original drawing or writing. Where records for the site are missing it is sometimes possible to glean information from plans for other sites. At Painshill, for example, Mark Laird discovered and used an evergreen planting plan drawn by Lord Petre for the Duke of Norfolk in 1737/8 when planning the replanting of the amphitheatre.

The changing nomenclature of plants and the use of common names make identification difficult, and it is often necessary to compare plant descriptions and paintings for identification. Luckily the elaborate, crossword clue-like hunt to verify plant names can increasingly be eliminated by reference to recent research work by others, but even where plants can be identified, it may be difficult or impossible to find a source of supply. Only nine of the original thirty varieties of holly grown by Charles Hamilton at Painshill have been recovered for the replanting. In growing fruit the early American colonists found that every seedling gave a new variety, and needless to say not all survived. Research work should therefore include checking the availability of plants of the correct period.

Survey

AERIAL PHOTOGRAPHY

A full field survey should be carried out before taking any design or restoration decisions. Aerial photography is an invaluable preliminary measure for all but the smallest gardens both because, by the use of photogrammetry, the existing site can be mapped, and also because aerial photographs often show evidence of earlier garden layouts, particularly in certain weather conditions – a dry summer or under a light cover of snow. These can then be confirmed by archaeological investigation. Most of Britain is covered by aerial photographs.[1]

FIELD SURVEY

In a field survey the intentions of earlier designers may be gleaned from particular features of the area such as rivers, views or buildings. Specialist knowledge is required for the dating of architectural elements including walls, gates and sculpture. Correlation with accounts can only be made if the workmanship and materials are fully understood. Trees can be dated very approximately by the size of their girth, but since growing conditions are subject to variation this is often wildly inaccurate. A test bore and ring count will be necessary for accurate dating. The intended shape of the tree can be determined by evidence of clipping or pollarding at the time of transplantation. Indicator species, such as the wild hyacinth (*Endymion nonscriptus*), or diversity in a plant community will sometimes give an idea of age and may provide clues as to previous management.

ARCHAEOLOGY

New techniques have been developed for preliminary archaeological survey work. In America these investigative techniques are known as 'non-destructive archaeology' and include proton magnometry, electro-magnometry, infra-red photography and radar. In Britain a resistivity test, recently developed at Surrey University, was used during archaeological investigation at Painshill Park. The electrical resistance of the ground can be plotted over a given area. Damp ground has a lower electrical resistance than dry ground and the presence of structures hidden under the surface can therefore be detected by the difference in the resistivity readings. Usually the surrounding soil retains more moisture, but at Painshill it was the brick foundations of the Turkish tent which retained more moisture and gave the lower readings.

Non-destructive archaeological techniques are useful in locating features known to exist, or in indicating the presence of below ground structures, but for accurate investigation excavation is necessary, and is unavoidably both time-consuming and expensive. Archaeology in gardens, particularly in those which are no more than two or three hundred years old, is new and the possibilities exciting, but cross-checking with historical records is vital if it is to be of genuine use. It is possible, for example, for the archaeologist to identify the genus and sometimes the species of plants from the seed and pollen in a soil sample, but not to determine whether the plants were actually cultivated, or merely weeds, or even seeds blown in from outside. Archaeology can be much more accurate in uncovering and dating the building or infilling of features such as ponds, paths and garden buildings. Differences in the soil, its colour and texture, evidence of compaction or of wood fibres, may indicate earth banks or terraces, post holes, or even the way in which the ground has been cultivated. At Monticello post holes indicating the line of the fence, known to have been erected in Jefferson's day, have been carefully excavated. At Painshill, in an area burrowed by rabbits, the discovery of a 'post hole' was greeted with some scepticism. In test digs at Castle Bromwich, Birmingham, undulating cultivation lines in the vertical soil section have given rise to various theories. The most likely explanation is that they indicate a nursery area where plants, perhaps trees, were grown on, since the cultivation furrows must have remained the same for some years in order to leave a detectable mark in the soil.

RECORDING INFORMATION

Detailed archaeological investigation may be continued as part of the restoration process after the general field survey is complete. Finds do not always confirm early suppositions from the field survey, and therefore a degree of flexibility should be allowed in the design proposals. The interpretation and clear recording of survey information is essential both as a historical record and in order to facilitate design decisions. There are standard methods of recording tree surveys and basic site information, but for the purpose of conservation one of the most useful techniques is the preparation of overlays on a basic plan to show the historic development of a site at various stages, and to identify which features date from each period. Overlays frequently give an immediate and clear indication either of the most important period in a garden's history or of the various contributions from each period to the whole, and therefore whether the garden should be actively restored to a certain date or dates, or whether a gentler method of conservation through maintenance and upkeep is preferable.

New techniques using computers to record information can be extremely useful at this stage. Once set up, a programme can be used for continuous recording of the restoration process and subsequent maintenance. The American National Park Service uses an automated mapping and computer-aided design system developed at Boston University in managing the Olmsted National Historic Site. The basic software package is relatively inexpensive and operates on a Mackintosh computer. Computers have also been used for historic surveys by Travers Morgan Planners, notably at Hampton Court, London.

Design

FINANCIAL PLANNING

Design decisions for conservation will depend not only on historical research and survey, but also on the possible sources of financial aid. Since grants are often available for specific elements of restoration such as planting or the repair of garden buildings, each design proposal must be considered, not only on its straightforward conservation merits, but also in relation to potential funding. Financial projections for the expected income and maintenance costs must be made when assessing the feasibility of conservation proposals. A proposal to return a garden not only to a form as close to the original as possible, but also to the degree of use enjoyed in the past, may be an attractive one, but where this means a select number of visitors it may not be financially viable.

The Société Civile du Désert de Retz are hoping that the Désert can retain the atmosphere of the private pleasure ground enjoyed by François de Monville and his friends in the eighteenth century. They are looking at ways in which entrance to the Désert can be facilitated by means of selling an entrance card for 'les amis du Désert' which would allow a certain number of visits per year when the garden is ready to open to visitors in 1993, rather than encouraging wide general use by the public in the manner of a public park, for which the surrounding Forest of Marly is already available. It is more usual however to seek to attract as many visitors as possible in order to maximise income, but additional visitors can also increase costs. The final design proposals should represent a balancing act, juggling the potential number of visitors with the consequent need for facilities and the increased burden on maintenance.

MANAGEMENT PLANNING AND IMPLEMENTATION

The design scheme must take account of a feasible programme for implementation and should include a management plan. Management covers planning and policy decisions and the organisation of staff and equipment to integrate use with efficient maintenance. Maintenance involves routine operations for upkeep such as weeding, mowing or pruning which are performed to a daily, weekly or seasonal timetable. It is rare for all restoration work to be undertaken at the outset and, even where it is, it will still be necessary to plan for the replacement of planting at intervals in the future. At Blenheim, Cobham Resource Consultants have prepared a restoration plan which allows for the management of planting on a rotational basis after the initial ten-year phase of work. The exact timing of replanting may depend on unforeseen considerations such as disease, storm damage, or unexpected demands on resources, but the plan serves as a guide for future maintenance and enables the owner to budget ahead for major replacement costs, for example the clear felling and replanting of an avenue at the end of the trees' normal lifespan.

Management plans cannot cover all eventualities even in the short term. Often archaeological research reveals unexpected evidence, and both design decisions and management plans need to be reviewed accordingly. Nevertheless it is essential for the continuity of a project, given that the management itself is bound to change over time, that the broad outline of a management programme is clearly set out. A management plan should be based on an analysis of the main garden components and their condition, and of the existing maintenance methods and techniques, and staffing levels. It should be positive in approach, covering the future phased renewal of major features, and the timing of major expenditure on repairs or replanting, and planning for both the present and future impact of public access and any other commercial ventures. There should be a clear statement of the aims of the plan in the short, medium and long term. Just as one can look at the long history of a garden which is the subject of conservation, so too one should look well into its future.

A management plan must take into consideration the team which will implement the design and restoration, and the subsequent changes anticipated. The implementation of a conservation or restoration project is usually carried out either by the permanent garden staff under the supervision of a head gardener with specialist contractors brought in where necessary, or by a special restoration team, such as those sponsored by government through the Manpower Services Commission and Employment Training schemes at Painshill and Castle Bromwich, or by outside contractors. Where the restoration team is divorced from subsequent maintenance or where outside contractors are employed for much of the work, the need for a long-term management plan is obvious. If implementation and maintenance are carried out by the same team it may be possible to rely on short-term maintenance plans within an agreed management policy. The National Trust have a management team of three, a gardens adviser, the land agent and the head gardener, for each garden, who meet every six months and decide on the maintenance programme on a twice yearly basis, but while this may work well within the structure of a large organisation, it does not allow for long-term planning and might be cumbersome if there were unexpected changes of staff.

It is always preferable to use permanent staff to carry out restoration work, both because it is difficult to find general contractors who have experience in conservation, and to ensure continuity. There is a much greater degree of motivation for garden staff if they are involved with a project from its inception through to the establishment of a regular maintenance routine. Even where it is not practical to use permanent garden staff for restoration work the head gardener should be involved in the project as early as possible. Successful conservation depends as much on upkeep as on the initial restoration measures, and it is essential to work hand in hand with those who will be responsible for maintenance and to capture their enthusiasm, understanding and co-operation. The practical observations of a head gardener are invaluable in deciding an adequate, overall management plan.

Maintenance and management

3

Planthouses force Italian heat
On melon, pepper, peach and vine
And horticultural conceit
Perfects a Scottish aubergine.
Douglas Dunn

The cultivation of gardens has always been a struggle against climate. From the water features of Persian and Moorish gardens to the planthouses and hot, flued walls of Scottish ones, garden design has demonstrated a preoccupation with the adaptation of the environment to enable diverse plants to thrive. The maintenance of gardens which are heavily dependent on labour or energy is no longer as practical today as it once was, because resources have diminished as costs have increased. The demise of the kitchen garden has been one inevitable result. In many gardens upkeep is only feasible if alternatives to traditional methods of maintenance can be found. The use of irrigation systems, modern equipment and machinery, and even herbicides and pesticides must all be considered.

Maintenance planning

Maintenance should be the result of a sensible plan of action based on the style of the garden. Labour normally accounts for seventy to eighty per cent of garden maintenance costs, so the use of staff should be as efficient as possible. Economics, and especially reductions in staffing levels, have threatened the character of many gardens through the elimination or modification of some of their more labour-intensive features, but modern aids can ensure adequate maintenance of quite intricate and formal designs despite a reduction in manpower. Nevertheless, in some cases where the restoration of an original planting scheme is deemed necessary to the integrity of the design, it is impossible to devise a satisfactory maintenance system. The original planting may have been somewhat experimental in terms of its suitability for the location, and successful cultivation of the same plants on the site therefore may prove problematic. The problems are compounded by current expectations of the quality of plants as we have become accustomed to a wide variety of plants and hybrids, selected and bred for ever bigger and better forms and flowers.

Planting design

The dahlia walk which the National Trust are replanting at Biddulph Grange is an example where it is difficult to envisage successful maintenance because the walk, although sheltered from wind, will be equally shielded for much of the day from sun by its walls and high yew hedges – not an ideal situation for dahlias. When reinstating an original design though, the attempt itself can be educational, and a compromise eventually reached either by growing only those varieties which prove to be tolerant of the situation, and settling for less variety in the planting, or by substituting more suitable modern forms, or different flowers of the correct period. Historical accuracy in such a case is bound to be compromised since there is no way of knowing how the early planting was adapted from the original scheme in order to compensate for losses.

Where it is appropriate, maintenance can be simplified by use of botanical species and cultivars of hardy plants which need less attention, and live longer, than hybrid forms, although they may be less colourful or striking in appearance. Hybrids often need a high level of input to produce the effect for which they are bred. Native species originating from the wild usually outlive both hybrids and cultivars. In Britain the gean (*Prunus avium*) will live for over one hundred years whereas the Japanese cherries commonly have a healthy life of only forty to fifty years.

In horticulture the prime objective of a maintenance programme is for amenity and pleasure. There is little or no production aspect or profit motive in comparison with agriculture, and consequently the need for new maintenance techniques seems less urgent and very little research has been done on the maintenance problems in gardens. Too little is known of the effects of competition and companionship among cultivated plants compared with the ecology of plant communities in the wild. Different associations or groupings of plants may help each other and reduce maintenance. Close planting in herbaceous borders can

36 and 37   There is no maintenance without gardeners – at Herrenhausen (above) and La Pretaia (below). Staff wages usually account for seventy to eighty per cent of maintenance costs

reduce the need for staking. Aphids are supposed to be repelled by garlic planted in association with roses. Diseases such as rose black spot or dry mildew may be combated by planting more resistant plant varieties, and a mulch of lawn clippings on rose beds can also help to reduce the incidence of black spot.

New techniques

The diversity of size and style and the range of plants and plant associations in gardens give rise to problems in achieving skilled and careful maintenance as there is limited scope for the safe and effective application of new machinery and chemicals. Conservation bodies which have resources to distribute between many gardens can at least hope to maintain one example of a certain garden type in a traditional manner, as the National Trust aim to do if they find a suitable kitchen garden, but, for owners and managers of individual gardens, finding the best methods of maintenance to serve the interests of conservation is often a matter of trial and error.

It is a pity that there is not more pooling of information on particular maintenance problems in historic gardens. Tom Wright's book, *Large Gardens and Parks*, printed in 1982, is an excellent general source of reference, but managers and head gardeners should be aware of the ways in which similar problems to their own have been tackled elsewhere, and with what success. For this reason research at the design stage should examine the maintenance implications of the techniques employed in other garden restorations. The restoration at Het Loo employs plastic sheeting under the gravel of all the parterres, and yet at Herrenhausen plastic sheeting was found to encourage the growth of algae, thus making frequent cleaning or replacement of the gravel necessary. It didn't suppress the worst menace, Schachtelhalm (*Equisetum*) which, thanks to roots as long as one and a half metres, emerges in the box hedges whence it is particularly difficult to remove.

Keeping records

Better access to information on the tackling of maintenance problems peculiar to the conservation of gardens would benefit all those involved. In the individual garden a cross referencing system of recording information, which facilitates quick checking both on the previous maintenance of certain areas, and the handling of different maintenance operations, would be invaluable. The National Trust's system of six-monthly reports is adequate for the forward planning of the maintenance schedule, but ploughing chronologically backwards through reports for information on one particular item is at best clumsy. For easy reference the information from reports can be used to update a computer system, or a simple card index file can be kept. Each card should record the type of operation carried out, the area of the garden, and the date, with comments on success or failure and the reasons for these results. The system can also be used to record planting and problems concerning the management of visitors and the solutions tried. Such a record will not only assist in the future management of the garden but also provide a fund of information for research which, if correlated, will aid the conservation movement as a whole.

Glasshouses

The longer-term management implications of a restoration are important, especially when money is usually available in the form of grants for restoration but not for maintenance. Nowadays the architectural elements of a garden lack the continuous care of skilled masons and craftsmen which was provided in the past, and decay is aggravated by pollution and vandalism. These built elements, usually the first to be restored because they readily attract grants, can be a drain on the resources available for maintenance, and their continued care and use should be carefully considered. Glasshouses, for example, are seldom justifiable in terms of cost alone, but work in them can be done in bad weather, ensuring a supply of the right stock to a garden where there are more unusual plants in cultivation. They are important to job satisfaction, attracting skilled horticultural staff, so many of whom go into commercial nurseries or research. Now that the importance of using historic varieties is more widely recognised, and the 'cleaning' of them has become possible, the production of stock is likely to play an increasingly significant role in the maintenance of historic gardens.

Staff

The need for staff to be fully conversant, and happy with the tools and techniques employed in maintenance cannot be over-emphasised. Capital expenditure on equipment is totally wasted if machinery lies idle because a gardener prefers to stick to the methods he knows and has been using for years. Adequate training and protective clothing must also be allowed for in the maintenance budget, and increments in rates of pay for skilled operators of larger items of machinery or of spray equipment, where this is normal practice. Where differentials in wages exist between the public and private sectors to the detriment of attracting and keeping staff, as in the American National Park Service or the German state administrations, it is even more important to consider overall job satisfaction. In a garden like that of Schloss Linderhof in Bavaria, remote and under snow for seven months of the year, this may be well-nigh impossible – only a certain type of person would be happy in such a situation – but in general the care of a heritage garden can usually provide reasonable job security and a greater variety of work and level of interest for the average gardener, which may go some way towards compensating for lower rates of pay.

Visitors

The use of the garden by visitors and the way in which visits may affect the deployment of staff must also be taken into account in planning a maintenance regime. Where gardens were, historically, for private use and enjoyment there was perhaps little conflict between use and maintenance. Indeed, seeing a gardener at work may have added to the pleasure of a leisurely stroll through the grounds. The number of visitors which many gardens now have to accommodate however, can impede a gardener's work. Temporary barriers such as the chains used to seal off paths from visitors at Giverny can help to solve the physical problems, but gardeners are sometimes required to explain aspects of their work or of the planting, or even to act as guides. While this may add to the satisfaction to be gained from the job, it is also time-consuming and allowance should be made.

Maintenance operations

Weed control

There are three main divisions of regular maintenance, tree and hedge work, the care of grassed areas, and weed control. Weeding may take up to forty-five per cent of staff time so it is a large item in any maintenance budget. Weeds, apart from detracting from the appearance of a garden, compete for water and nutrients and can dramatically reduce the growth of garden plants. May and June are the critical months for weed control, when the main flush of weed growth coincides with the extension growth of ornamental plants, so diligent weeding should be kept up during this period until the competition for growth is less crucial.

The soil is a reservoir of weed seeds; 'one year's seeding, seven years' weeding'. If seeding can be prevented and the ground cultivated twice a year, the number of weed seeds can be reduced by about thirty per cent per year, but, since the population of weed seeds in the top fifteen millimetres of soil has been found to be as high as fifty thousand seeds per square metre, it may take eleven years to reduce the number to one hundred seeds per square metre, which is rated as weed-free soil.[1] Perennial weeds also have a persistent means of survival, notably by creeping root systems. When preparing the ground for the replacement of planting, one solution to the problem of clearing weeds is to apply a herbicide, providing that the soil can then be left for a sufficient length of time for its effect to dissipate before replanting.

Herbicides

Where permitted, herbicides can also be used in regular garden maintenance and weed control. There are three main types: contact, translocated and residual herbicides. Contact herbicides (e.g. paraquat) kill only those parts of the plants with which they come into contact, and are therefore mainly used in a spray for controlling seedling or annual weeds. Translocated herbicides (e.g. glysophate) are absorbed by the leaves into the sap of the plant and thus transmitted to kill all parts of the plant. They take longer to be effective. Residual herbicides (e.g. simazine) are usually applied to the soil surface where they prevent the germination of seedlings.

Herbicides are usually applied in spray or granular form. Proper protective clothing must be worn when using them, and their application, particularly when spraying, should be carried out by a trained operator. There seems to be no apparent damage to soil structure, provided the herbicides are applied at the recommended rates, and where herbicides have been in use for a number of years they encourage the growth of a moss layer which can be attractive. Their impact on the wider environment, however, may be more damaging, and many plants are susceptible to their use. Particular care must be taken with annuals, perennials and bulbs since many of them have similar forms to the weeds which are the object of attack.

The use of herbicides is increasingly frowned upon; they are almost totally banned in West Germany, and strictly controlled elsewhere. They will never replace hand and mechanical weeding, particularly in gardens where many susceptible plants are grown. Even where they are permitted, the justification for using herbicides, especially in historic restoration work, is being questioned, and other effective methods of weed control are being sought. According to Dr John Davidson of the WRO, Oxford,

The full potential of herbicides cannot be developed if they are merely seen as alternatives to the hoe. They enable and indeed require a complete reappraisal of land management.

In a historic garden such a radical revision of the approach to management is probably less appropriate than in other areas of amenity horticulture.

Alternative methods of weed control

Two of the main operations which might benefit from alternative methods of weed control are the preparation of the ground for planting and the maintenance of gravel surfaces. At the Palace of Falkland in Fife, Scotland, where a new garden was laid out in 1947 to a design by Percy Cane, the ground had been effectively cleared by its use as a potato patch during the war. Presumably in pursuit of a similar result, Sir John Clerk of Penicuik recommends in his 'Notes' that potatoes and turnips be planted under young trees. Perhaps this method of clearing the ground might profitably be re-employed today. In West Germany, although the use of herbicides to eliminate weeds from gravel is disapproved, the use of a mechanical flame thrower is not, despite the inevitable air pollution. The effectiveness of the machine is, however, limited since it will burn off the surface vegetation but cannot penetrate to the root system. At Herrenhausen garden staff are experimenting with a vibration machine which rakes and smooths, and has the added advantage of assisting drainage. Plastic sheeting can also be used, although it has disadvantages which are discussed elsewhere.[2]

Hand weeding and mulching

Where cultivation tools are used, care must be taken not to damage the roots of ornamental plants. Hoeing will kill weeds by the shallow disturbance of the soil provided there is sufficient dry weather to prevent re-establishment. Forking will be necessary for deep rooted perennial weeds. Close planting or mulching will help smother annual weed growth, and lawn clippings can economically be used in this way, saving some trips to the compost heap into the bargain. Other materials, for example garden compost, shredded bark, straw or fresh sawdust, can be used as mulches, but cost (including the need for a supplementary nitrogen dressing in the case of straw or sawdust mulches) and appearance must be carefully considered. Where the main attraction of a heritage garden is a large plant collection, the extensive use of mulching may well be justified, but in situations where the historic accuracy of

38 Pitmedden – a stripey lawn can visually destroy a historic setting

39 Hedge cutting from moveable scaffolding at Hidcote

the planting is a major consideration, mulches may be inappropriate unless there is a historic precedent for their use. In many areas hand weeding will remain the only satisfactory method of weed control. It does at least have a therapeutic value for the gardener, and the benefit of aiding the observation and understanding of the plants.

Grass cutting

During the growing season, the regular cutting and maintenance of grassed areas to maintain their appearance and to cope with pedestrian traffic is one of the more demanding maintenance tasks. Few gardens are without an expanse of grass, and an assumption that such areas should be maintained as close mown lawn is fairly general, so that consideration of the care of grassed areas in a manner appropriate to a historic garden has been sorely neglected until recently. Rudi and Joy Favretti have done much to introduce discussion of this subject in their book, *Landscapes and Gardens for Historic Buildings*, published in America. Stripey lawns are relatively modern – the lawn mower was not widely used until the 1860s – and insensitively mown grass can visually destroy a historic setting. At Falkland, the stripey lawn is not inappropriate to the design of the garden itself, but it jars as the setting for a fifteenth-century palace, adding to the modern impression of island beds floating in a vast sea of grass. The National Trust has acknowledged the need for a different approach at Studley Royal where the grass around the ruined Fountains Abbey is no longer close mown, but is allowed to grow to two or three inches in length and cut high. A reciprocating cutter bar or sicklebar mower produces an effect similar to hand scything since the machine is forward mounted and does not flatten the grass before cutting.

Grazing

It is a pity that at Fountains Abbey the ultimate solution to the problem of grass maintenance, grazing, cannot be employed once again. The number of visitors makes this impractical, but in other situations the reintroduction of grazing may be more feasible. Income from rents can be offset against the cost of other areas of maintenance. Several factors must be taken into account: the local demand for grazing land, the need for adequate drainage and fencing or hedging, the protection of trees, and whether grazing will provide adequate maintenance. Different animals not only graze differently but also cause differing degrees of wear. Cattle and horses rapidly churn wet ground to mud, and are liable to cause root damage to mature trees through compaction. Deer cause a great deal of tree damage, and in a limited areas horses will chew the bark of mature trees. Sheep do less physical damage but are more selective grazers, leaving tussocks of rougher grasses rather than a smooth greensward behind them. If sheep graze the same pasture over a long period they reinfect themselves with their own parasites. The use of grazing is therefore most worthwhile over large areas if a clean grazing system, rotating sheep with cattle and horses on a three to four year cycle, is possible. Geese are efficient grazers for smaller areas, but their droppings are unsightly and, in too restricted a space, they can paddle the ground.

Grass cutting machinery

Grass cutting machinery is available in all sizes and types – cylinder, rotary, flail and sicklebar mowers or strimmers – to suit different jobs or areas. The number of cuts should be determined by the length of grass required related to growing conditions. More cuts will be required in a wet growing season, but cutting does not of itself encourage grass growth. The use of slower growing grasses in the seed mix can help reduce the amount of cutting necessary, but on average close mown turf will require cutting twenty-five to thirty times a year. Cylinder mowers are most commonly used for areas of close mown formal lawn, but they are easily damaged by sticks and stones if these are not removed before cutting. A spin trimmer is far quicker than hand edge cutting, but only in the hands of a willing gardener!

Grass clippings

Much effort can be saved by leaving the grass clippings on the ground if the grass is cut short. If the grass is grown higher, the clippings can be used for mulching. Since periods of rapid growth of both grasses and weeds coincide it is possible to gain the best of both worlds by mulching with grass clippings at the height of the season, and otherwise leaving the clippings to return nutrients to the soil. Clippings have other uses. Grass paths are subject to considerable wear and tear if the number of visitors is high, particularly after a wet summer. At Crathes one year, after much rain, worn patches of grass were given a coarse sand dressing to prevent them turning to mud, and cleverly disguised with fresh grass clippings until visitors numbers dropped and re-seeding could take place.

Drainage

Adequate drainage is crucial to the survival of grass under heavy pedestrian traffic and wet conditions. In older gardens grass paths covering earlier gravel ones have been found to wear much better as a consequence of good drainage. Dry conditions too, in conjunction with heavy use, can cause worn patches, although in general the effect of drought, turning green lawn to brown, is only temporary. Moveable barriers to direct the passage of pedestrians away from worn areas, thus giving the grass a chance to recover, or the use of duckboards at points of particularly heavy wear, such as the entrance to an expanse of lawn, are useful aids to avoiding the necessity for re-seeding. Periodic surface aeration of the turf will also be necessary. For small areas this can be done by hand with a garden fork.

Restoring hedges

Old and overgrown yew, holly, laurel or privet hedges can often be restored by cutting back hard to the trunk and allowing new growth to develop. It is preferable to treat one side at a time in successive years and to follow with a mulch and fertiliser dressing. Simple topiary forms can sometimes also be treated in this way although if new growth fails to develop there is no alternative to replacement. For hedges, if plants are spaced sufficiently closely, the new growth of neighbouring plants can usually be trained to fill any gaps left by individual plants which do not respond after cutting back. If the spacing is wider, replacement plants may be necessary, but new plants will be overshadowed and their growth may be inhibited to the extent that the hedge remains gappy. In this case complete replanting of the hedge may be the best option. Other conifer species cannot be treated by cutting back, and box is much better replanted using cuttings from the overgrown plants.

Hedge cutting

For routine hedge cutting mechanical aids are invaluable, but there are drawbacks. It is impossible to get as close a cut with machinery as by hand, and for most topiary work hand cutting is the only answer. It is often possible to alternate hand and machine cutting so that the hedge is kept tight. At Pitmedden, where the box hedges are cut twice a year, one of the four parterres is cut by hand each time so that each parterre is close cut by hand every other year. At Crathes Castle the bulk of the old yew hedges are cut using machines, but the more intricate topiary work is done by hand. Yew needs cutting only once a year, but it takes two hours to cut just one of the spherical topiary shapes so hedge cutting takes up considerable staff time. The collection of clippings can, however, be speeded by using a suction cleaner. The pruning of pleached limes is usually done, as at Herrenhausen, by hand. Special scaffolding on rollers is available to facilitate the cutting of high hedges, and at Herrenhausen a lift is rented for the tallest limes. These are cut every four years, but the sides only, not the top. It is essential always to allow hedging plants to grow to the intended height of the hedge before cutting the leaders.

Alternatives to hedge cutting

The use of growth retardants is sometimes mooted as a method of labour saving on hedge cutting. It is doubtful whether their use does in fact achieve any greater reduction in labour than the use of mechanical hedge cutting equipment. Certainly, unless it results in considerable savings in manpower, the use of further chemicals can scarcely be justified. The other alternative, replanting with a species which needs less clipping, usually runs counter to the aims of conservation but. where the labour problem is acute, and a substitute true to the period of the garden can be selected, it may be acceptable. The planting of smaller topiary forms in yew or holly rather than box, for example, would represent a substantial saving.

Trees – retention and replacement

Garden conservationists have often gone to elaborate lengths to retain individual trees of a venerable age even where, in normal circumstances, their condition would be enough to dictate immediate felling. This may be justified where an individual tree has historic importance, is a remnant of the original planting or a rare specimen, or where the loss of the tree would fundamentally change the whole character of the design. It is difficult to conceive the beauty of the garden of the Villa Lante at Bagnaia without the shade of the planes over the central terraces of the water garden, and yet to continue to conserve these trees is only to put off the inevitable. It must be remembered that it is only a matter of time before newly planted trees will mature in their turn to provide the necessary shade. In the case of the now incomplete roundels of holm oaks in the centre of the garden at La Pretaia, it is harder to understand why some attempt has not been made to plant new trees in the gaps so that loss of shade will not be total when the old trees eventually go. Perhaps it is sufficient to preserve the unsullied beauty of mature trees for as long as possible, but, in a garden where there are frequent visitors, the risk of retaining trees which are in a blatantly dangerous state is a parlous one.

Causes of tree loss and damage

The replacement of trees forms a major part of conservation, and especially of the initial restoration process. Recent storms in Britain have been a forceful reminder that trees too have a limited lifespan, even if longer than our own. Snow can also cause severe damage, breaking branches under the pressure of its weight. Less obvious is the damage caused by drought. It takes some years for the effect of drought to be felt, usually by the loss of greater numbers of trees in high winds after their growth has been weakened by an inordinate lack of moisture. Root damage can be caused by compaction of the soil round a tree, either through the use of machinery or from dumping material during the process of restoration itself, or even by the trampling feet of numerous visitors. It should be possible to avoid the use of heavy machinery too close to mature trees and to fence off the area under the tree canopy if necessary or, where visitors present the problem, to use a heavy mulch or a deterrent ground cover planting.

Replanting trees – size and staking

Trees grow best when planted as young as possible, as seedlings or whips, but it may be desirable to replace a particular feature, such as an avenue, with larger, standard or half-standard, trees. Standard trees seem especially prone to vandalism. Careful staking will minimise the risk of loss, particularly from malicious breaking of the stem, but will not eliminate the problem. Trees can still walk if assisted! It is common practice, when planting standard trees, to use heavy stakes tied into the base of the crown, but holding the stem rigid makes it more prone to snapping under pressure above the tie. Trees which are tied at the top of the stem are also more susceptible to wind blow when the stake is finally removed. The stem will strengthen naturally as well as proffer better resistance if allowed to bend more freely. Research indicates that stakes are best tied at one-third of the clear height of the stem during the first growing season while the roots establish, and should be removed at the start of the second growing season after planting so that the stem is free to develop naturally before the onset of autumn and winter gales.[3]

Maintenance and management

Elaborate methods to retain individual trees

40 Propped – La Pretaia

41 Bolted – Veitshöcheim

42 Metal ties – Castello

43 Rainwater chute – Monticello

Tree protection

Large tree guards offer better protection against vandalism than staking, as well as being essential where there are grazing cattle or horses which can both cause damage to mature trees. Young trees need protection from deer and rabbits. Where adequate fencing is impractical, spiral guards can be used on newly planted trees. Tree shelters in the form of plastic tubes can give similar protection when fitted over seedlings. the shelter acts as a mini-greenhouse, encouraging strong vertical growth, but, since the tube is rigid, it has the same effect as that of tall stakes on standard trees, preventing the natural strengthening of the stem, and should be removed and replaced with a spiral guard as soon as possible. Fencing is much more cost effective than tree guards in protecting large areas of tree planting, although where it is a permanent rather than a temporary measure, the visual intrusion on a historic landscape if it is not well sited can be a severe drawback. It is often hard to hide – deer fencing for example needs to be eight feet high to prevent jumping, but nevertheless at Biltmore it is largely successfully concealed by the woodland itself. At Monticello there is a paradox in the opposition to the replacement of Jefferson's ten foot high paling fence because of its appearance and the blocking of the view although it is desirable in both practical and restoration terms.

Trees – transplanting and establishment

Good ground preparation and careful treatment of trees during transplanting and the first subsequent growing season is crucial to successful establishment. The roots should not be allowed to dry out, although young, deciduous trees can be transplanted bareroot during the winter months. Trees which are container grown can be planted outwith the normal planting season but, in general, late autumn is the ideal time for planting, before the first frosts of winter, or, failing that, in early spring before the growing season starts. Watering is vital since some moisture loss and reduction of the rootball is inevitable during transplantation. A good soaking is needed and can be given by bucket or hose and, over larger areas, from a water tank. An area of at least one metre in diameter around the tree's stem should be kept weed-free in the first year in order to reduce competition for both moisture and nutrients.[4] It is also important, when trees are rootballed, to break the surrounding hessian even though it will rot in time, in order to prevent compaction and waterlogging around the roots – a seemingly obvious piece of advice, but for many a dead, dying or windblown tree this simple step has been overlooked.

Ground preparation, drainage and irrigation

Attention should be paid to ground preparation, particularly after heavy compaction by machinery. Air is as important to root growth as water so it is necessary to break up the soil to a depth sufficient to allow adequate drainage below the roots. In some situations the installation of permanent drainage may be necessary. Watering and irrigation are on the other side of the coin from drainage. Both should be considered together when preparing the ground for planting to decide whether some sort of permanent system is desirable. Irrigation has become necessary to the survival of historic planting schemes in many gardens where, in the past, the numbers of staff employed allowed hand watering in dry weather. Sometimes an irrigation system already exists although the pipes may have corroded, or the water source have dried up or been diverted to other uses such as domestic or industrial water supply. Such a system once supplied the walled garden at Biltmore and, of course, many gardens in hotter climates were designed around the channelling of water.

Irrigation systems

The reinstatement or installation of irrigation should be planned with regard to its condition, the available water supply, the head of water or necessity for pumping, and whether a permanent system can be justified by long periods of drought. For intermittent dry spells the capital cost of a permanent system may be disproportionately high and a moveable system prove a more cost effective alternative. There are several different types of irrigation systems, sprinklers or rotary sprays, which require an adequate head of water or a pump to operate effectively, and trickle feed systems using perforated piping, which operate from a low pressure supply. The drawback to overhead systems is the increase in moisture loss through evaporation, but for permanent systems, low sprays can keep the evaporation loss to a minimum.

Pruning and thinning

Operations such as pruning and thinning are essential to keep a planting scheme viable. The pruning of trees in the great Baroque formal gardens had the express intention of making the trees appear permanently young. Original planting plans in themselves seldom reveal the full story, what type of maintenance was intended and to what effect, although, if planting is still extant, a detailed vegetation survey can provide clues as to early pruning and training. The feasibility of the concept behind any planting design is as much dependent on its subsequent care as on the planting itself. Often much of the interest generated by the restoration of planting lies in seeing the whole process repeated as it was originally conceived and executed, but it is sometimes advantageous to treat certain areas of planting differently, albeit with the same end result in view. It may be desirable to try to achieve full ground cover quickly, either to reduce weeding or so that the planting will act as a barrier, and to plant more thickly at first, thinning out later to the original plan.

Thinning is also an essential part of regular maintenance. Herbaceous plants will require thinning either by division of the rootstock, usually every three to five years, or by grubbing out some of the growth of the more invasive species. Where woodland regenerates naturally from seed, the selection, protection and thinning of seedlings will encourage successful regeneration. The thinning of shrubs can largely be achieved by pruning. Pruning is done for one of two purposes, either to train and keep the plant to a desired size and shape, or to prolong the life of an old or diseased plant. In the latter case, drastic cutting back, as for hedges, can renew the appearance of some old and overgrown shrubs, and often plays an early part in the restoration programme. Regular pruning for shaping or thinning can change a plant's natural shape in various ways. Removal of the lower branches will raise the crown and can be used to change a shrub into a small tree. Growth in the crown can be reduced by selective pruning out of shoots and branches. Lateral growth, as for pleached or wall-trained trees, can be encouraged by removing shoots which do not grow in the desired direction. Occasionally a plant develops strong vertical shoots, at odds with its general form, and these too should be pruned out.

Tree paints are no longer considered to be particularly beneficial in healing the wounds caused by pruning larger branches. Instead, the cut should be made as close as possible to the thicker ring of pressure growth at the base of the branch so that the growth of callous over the cut will eventually heal the wound. If the angle of the cut is near to the horizontal, so that there is a danger of water pooling in the wound before it is properly healed, then a nick can be made in the ring of pressure growth to discourage the formation of callous at that point and thus to allow drainage. Pruning can be carried out throughout the year, although periods of frost or that of active sap growth in the spring are best avoided. Late summer or autumn is the ideal time to prune most plants except for Prunus species which should be tackled in July or August.

Management and maintenance problems

Ponds and water features

Water features in many heritage gardens require specialist attention, and, in gardens such as Herrenhausen, permanent staff are employed on the technical side to keep the fountains and plumbing in working order. Besides the upkeep of basic plumbing, the main problems in dealing with water features concern the initial repair of leaks in artificial lakes and ponds, the encroachment of aquatic plants and silting up of the water supply, and the control of algae. At Painshill the dredging of the lake was a major operation which, together with the re-forming of the lake edge, was a task of sufficient magnitude to be put out to contract rather than tackled by the MSC team or by volunteers. For smaller areas of water, draining and digging may prove an economical alternative to dredging, and draining will of course be necessary where an artificial lining, usually clay bottoming, needs to be repaired or re-laid to prevent seepage.

The restoration of ponds and lakes can often spark opposition from nature conservationists. However, the successful incorporation of frog ramps into the construction of the new edge of the recently restored lake at Studley Royal, and the thriving of a community of rare newts despite the digging out of the pond at Castle Bromwich, testify that restoration projects need not be detrimental to other conservation interests. Clear water surfaces are important in formal gardens where water bodies, ponds and canals were designed as reflective surfaces. In larger water areas a balance between plants and clear water surface is necessary to fish and animal life. Reeds are best controlled by mechanical cutting of the beds. Floating plants can be removed by hand or skimmed off the surface. At Herrenhausen staff are experimenting with the use of copper sulphate to keep the water free from algae. Other chemical clearing agents are available, but like all chemicals must be used with the utmost care. For large bodies of water one alternative, which is so simple that it must be worth trying, is to dump a bale of straw in the water. The action of bacteria on the straw helps reduce enrichment of the water by removing nitrogen.

Pests and diseases

The treatment of pests and diseases is fraught with difficulty when it comes to alternatives to the application of chemicals. Gone are the days when a bevy of gardeners' apprentices might have handpicked greenfly from the roses or caterpillars from the cabbages, and some of the more serious diseases, especially those affecting trees or particular plant species can cause direct conflict with the aims of historic conservation unless they can be fully and effectively eliminated. In deciding on treatment consideration should first be given as to how serious the problem really is. Birds, slugs and mildew remove buds, chew leaves or make a plant unsightly but, in all but the worst years it may be acceptable to ignore them. Many diseases are aggravated by damp conditions, and ensuring sufficient ventilation around the roots may help to prevent them. Fungal diseases of plant roots are among the most serious and difficult to treat. For those which attack specific plants the usual treatment is to remove the diseased plants and to avoid replanting with the same species for several years until the soil is free from disease, but for conservationists dealing with historic planting layouts this solution runs counter to the aim of integrity in restoration. At Sissinghurst the sacrifice of the carpet of polyanthus under the hazel trees in the nuttery, and their replacement by other woodland species, when the soil became primula sick was to lose a stroke of genius in Vita Sackville-West's planting of the garden. There is, however, no point in replanting the same species in contaminated soil, so the only other alternative is to change or sterilise the soil.

Honey fungus (*Armillaria mellea*) is one of the commonest fungi to attack a wide variety of trees and shrubs. Some species – beech, oak, lime, yew and holly among them – are more resistant than others. The fungus needs dead woody tissue to survive so all tree stumps and roots should be removed from an infected area and burnt, together with as much as possible of the underground, black 'bootlace' strands of the rhizomorphs which are the principal means by which the fungus spreads to healthy plants. In isolated outbreaks it may be possible to prevent the spread of infection by sinking a vertical barrier of plastic sheeting into the ground to a depth of at least one metre. Where hedges succumb to the fungus, several healthy plants will need to be removed beyond those affected in order to contain the disease.

The scourge of Dutch elm disease appears to rise to epidemic proportions every few hundred years, a long natural cycle which so far has allowed the species to survive. On the whole the method of responding to the ravages of the latest outbreak has been to replant with the more resistant American elm or with another tree species altogether, either way hastening the demise of the elm as a feature of historic landscapes. Since the elm bark beetle carries the fungus only to reasonably mature trees, perhaps we should be more courageous in replanting native elms, especially the wych elm (*Ulmus glabra*) which grows freely from seed.

44 The ravages of Dutch elm disease

45 Anti-vandalism measures at Pitmedden – problem or cure?

Architectural features

In all aspects of the maintenance and repair of hard landscape features the best sources of knowledge are local craftsmen, where they still exist. Sometimes information on wrought or cast ironwork, stone balustrading, follies and garden ornament can be found in illustrated books, but often the reconstruction of built elements relies on the use of intelligent guesswork. It is usually possible to detect from the remnants of a path, for example, how it has been constructed, so that it can be repaired accordingly. The restoration of patterned paving can become an elaborate jigsaw puzzle. Just such a problem was painstakingly solved at Painshill when the floor of the Mausoleum was re-laid. In its original form, sculpture was often painted but, since old and weathered stone has its own attractions, there may be a reluctance to restore it to its original appearance. The repainting of the statues at Herrenhausen to restore them to a shimmering white imitation of marble was a courageous step in the 1960s. Attempts to repair sculpture are often crude and clumsy and, unless specialist advice can be afforded, it may well be preferable to accept the damage; broken can be better than flawed.

Theft

Garden ornaments have greatly increased in value recently, encouraging the problem of theft to rear its ugly head alongside that of vandalism. Where a piece is of sufficient value, its replacement with a copy, for both better security and conservation, may have to be considered. It is usually virtually impossible to install satisfactory alarm systems for garden ornaments but, as a matter of course, all garden ornaments should be photographed and catalogued. In Britain owners of any property open to the public can now join the Historic Houses Hotline, a telephone service set up to exchange information on suspicious visitors and stolen goods. Not only larger items, but plants and labels also, are subject to theft, and visitors can be remarkably brazen about taking cuttings. Having plants available for sale may counter temptation, but good policing is really the only solution. When parties are escorted by guides the problem is contained, but otherwise the working out of timetables so that gardeners are at work in vulnerable areas of the garden during opening times may help the situation. Many a gardener bemoans the extra burdens caused by visitors but without them few heritage gardens could justify their continuation. The integration of the use of a garden with its management is therefore vital in minimising the conflicts.

Vandalism

The involvement of local people in any proposed restoration helps spread understanding and interest. The more involved people become in a project, the more protective of it they are inclined to be, and this can be the best deterrent to vandalism. At Castle Bromwich the garden was protected by a security fence early on, but the involvement of local people on the MSC teams which worked on the restoration and in acting as guides has played an equal part in restoring the success of the project. Evidence of vandalism encourages further vandalism in snowballing, copycat actions, so prompt repair is important. At Barncluith the obvious neglect and destruction perpetuate a tragic situation as the garden, in its hidden position on the steep, wooded banks of the Avon, slowly but surely disintegrates. Physical preventative measures can be as ugly as the vandalism itself. The spikes and barbed wire above the gate in the south wall at Pitmedden greatly detract from the beauty of the wrought iron.

Litter

The other main problem that visitors bring in their wake is litter. In the Englischergarten in Munich it is reckoned that clearing up litter takes as much staff time as the actual care of the greenspace. At Biltmore too the problem has increased so that a notable amount of staff time must be spent on tidying up. There is no solution other than diligent supervision and picking up the debris. Well-placed litter bins are important, but if they intrude on the garden itself they seem to encourage carelessness by subtly changing the visitor's perception of the garden as a private place to that of a public park. It is sad that in either case littering should become even remotely acceptable but, as with vandalism, only by keeping the garden clean and tidy, so that there is no encouragement by example, will the problem be reduced.

Staffing

Naturally the demands on staff time increase with the influx of visitors in the summer months, just as the horticultural workload is at its most onerous. In the planning of any maintenance regime the level of staffing is crucial. Formal gardens require manicured maintenance and are bound to suffer if there is not a sufficient number of staff employed. The use of expensive equipment for summer tasks such as hedge and grass cutting, and irrigation, can therefore be justified if it helps to limit the workload to what can be managed by the usual complement of staff,

101

unless there is a source of cheap, summer labour available. Whether equipment is bought or hired will depend on the balance between capital and maintenance budgets and the magnitude and incidence of the task in hand. Jobs such as weeding, picking up litter, and the supervision of visitors can be managed by unskilled labour. Monticello benefits being able to employ students during the summer months, and at Herrenhausen extra staff are taken on from the ranks of the unemployed for a temporary period in the summer, but for most gardens it is important to plan to undertake as many tasks as possible during the winter months so that as much staff time as necessary can be devoted to essentially seasonal tasks. In the conservation of heritage gardens the aim of maintenance and management is to keep all the various elements, but especially the plants, in a healthy state for as long as is feasible. Manpower is the most important factor in achieving a satisfactory level of maintenance and, since labour costs are so high, staff time should be very carefully deployed.

Case studies

4

SCHLOSSGARTEN SCHWETZINGEN

Location, ownership and management

Schwetzingen is a small town not far from Heidelberg in the German state of Baden-Württemberg. The Schlossgarten is owned by the state and administered by the Oberfinanzdirektion Karlsruhe. The garden consists of seventy-two hectares of formal garden and landscape park laid out for the Elector Carl Theodor between 1748 and 1785. Like most of the other great German Baroque royal gardens the Schlossgarten at Schwetzingen is now open to the public, but it retains the atmosphere of a garden rather than a public park. This is due in part to its location and boundaries which allow the opening of just two entrances from the town, enabling good supervision and the charging of an entrance fee, and in part to the success of the restoration work already carried out. Visitors number some 500,000 per annum, but as many as 25,000 have been attracted to just one open air concert held in the garden. A management plan devised for the garden in 1970, initiated a programme of restoration under the able supervision of Hubert Wertz. Thirty people, gardeners, garden labourers and mechanics, are employed within the Schlossgarten for its care and maintenance.

Description and history

Schlossgarten Schwetzingen is designated both a Landschaftschutzgebeit and a Naturschutzgebeit (a Landscape and a Nature Conservation Area). It is of particular interest both because of the eclectic mixture of surviving garden features and because of the juxtaposition of the rigid geometry of the formal layout, designed by Johann Ludwig Petri and

Nicholas de Pigage, with the informal design of the surrounding park by Friedrich Ludwig von Sckell and Johann Michael Zeyher. Beyond the parterres of broderie and the formal bosquets a lake was created between 1766 and 1773. In 1777 von Sckell added the first 'English garden', that disparaged by William Beckford as 'a sunburnt, contemptible hillock, commanding a view of a serpentine ditch'. It was later extended by the naturalisation of the form of the lake, the building of the Temple of Mercury, begun in 1784, and the eventual completion of the Mosque with its smaller, mirror lake in 1795. Among its numerous other features, Schwetzingen boasts one of the few extant examples of a diorama as well as a Rococo theatre built in 1752.

Restoration and maintenance

Parterres

The first major part of the restoration was the reconstruction of the central broderie sections of the great circular parterre, between September 1973 and April 1974, according to a plan made by Petri in 1753. The other, grass sections of the parterre follow a plan by von Sckell but without the original plates-bandes. Subsequent research, concentrating on the *La Théorie et la Pratique du Jardinage* by Dézallier d'Argenville, enabled the planting of the plates-bandes round the central sections to be carried out in a historically correct mixture of species although, for reasons of maintenance and quality, modern varieties are used, and at present there are only two plantings, in spring and summer, rather than three. The parterre beds are weeded by hand, and a flame throwing machine is used on the gravel. For ease of maintenance a concrete edging separates the beds from the gravel. This should be hidden when the box hedges mature. The small cherub fountains have been reconstructed in epoxy resin.

Trees and hedges

After completion of the parterres, the replacement of the limes, which grossly overshadowed the new planting, was seen to be essential. The new trees were planted between 1982 and 1986. Notes written by von Sckell in 1792 instruct the cutting of overgrown trees so that they always appear young. The new limes will accordingly be grown to a height of eight metres, and pruned using a motorised saw and hedge clippers from a hydraulic ramp.

In the bosquets the smaller hedges are missing from the main cross allée

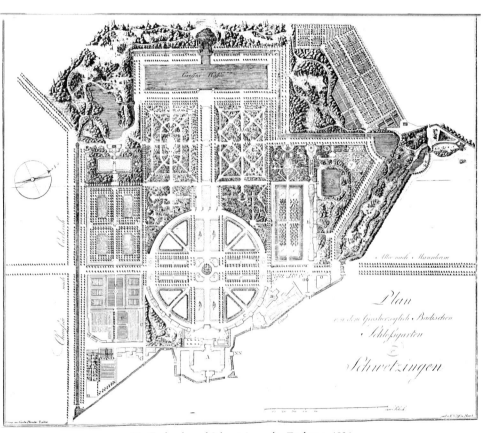

46   Early plan of Schwetzingen by Zeyher c. 1824

but, although they are shown by Dézallier, expert opinion is divided as to whether they were planted at Schwetzingen and therefore should be replaced. Other hedges, forming the boundaries to the compartments, have been restored to provide a green wall along the allées once again, but the restoration of the planting within the compartments has been hampered by opposition to tree felling from nature conservation activists. The ludicrous end result is the sight of many individual, overmature trees lopped and left, inevitably to die and at a greater risk to public safety. Much of the restoration work at Schwetzingen has involved the management, cutting back or replacement of overgrown planting. The plane trees, symbols of wisdom, have been replanted around the Temple of Minerva. The English garden was very overgrown in 1970. Some of the lime and plane trees brought back by von Sckell from England via Holland survived, and these have been retained where possible, but other planting has been cut back to open up the views and restore the design as it was originally conceived.

Water features

The canal in the English garden was restored in 1974, and in 1978 a new electric pump was installed to circulate water to the fountains. Plans were drawn up in 1986 for the reconstruction of the pond in the Arboretum to a plan by Pigage. New wooden retaining battens have been built on the original sandstone foundations. The restoration of the large pool below the stag fountains along the main axis is conceived as an important and integral part of the whole project. Research has uncovered numerous successive plans recording the changes to this area and verified that von Sckell's foundations still exist, but only the upper basin survives today in the form recorded by Zeyher in 1819. Of the stags, one is original, and the other made of composite stone.

Garden buildings

The Temple of Apollo was restored in 1985–6 and the aviary has been partly reconstructed and repainted and the perspective view with its waterfall to change the light on the picture and create a rainbow was under restoration in 1989. Future plans include the restoration of the mosque court which it is anticipated will cost seven million Deutsch-marks and take three years to complete. The orangery houses a lapidarium and in one of the circle buildings is an exhibition about the history of the garden and its restoration. It would be good to see some of the exhibition material incorporated into a new guidebook. The restoration has already done much to bring the Schlossgarten back from

47 The great circular parterre at Schwetzingen from the roof

48 Schloss and broderie with spring planting in the plates-bandes

public park to baroque garden, but in one respect its atmosphere will never be the same; a modern skyscraper obstructs the axis of the allée which once focused on the Elector's castle at Mannheim – a forceful reminder of the problems conservation faces.

GREAT GARDEN, HERRENHAUSEN

Location, ownership and management

The royal gardens of Herrenhausen are situated on the outskirts of Hanover. They consist of three gardens. The Great Garden itself, fifty-two hectares of formal, parterre and water gardens, was begun in 1666. To the north the Berggarten, originally a kitchen garden but early on used to house a collection of tropical plants, for which its first greenhouse was built in 1686, is now a botanic garden. The Georgengarten, a park laid out between 1820 and 1850 along the Herrenhausen avenue, the approach road to the palace constructed in 1726–7, is presently the subject of a conservation plan commissioned from outside consultants. The gardens became the property of the City Council in 1936 when the Great Garden was first restored. The Great Garden, together with the Berggarten, has its own administration which is responsible to the City Council's Department of Building. The annual maintenance budget is seven million Deutschmarks, divided equally between the two gardens, ninety per cent of which is provided by the City and ten per cent by the state of Niedersachsen. Another one and a half million Deutschmarks from the City Department of Building's budget goes towards the maintenance of the statues and buildings. Further funds for specific costs, such as the restoration of a building, have been raised by 'Aktionsausschuss Herrenhausen', a charitable body founded in 1962.

Visitor numbers are estimated at 7–800,000 per annum, with about 20,000 usually attracted to the Light Festivals although this figure has been as high as 35,000. Because of the difficulty of supervising the garden entrances and the extra costs this would involve in manning them, a charge is made only for entry to the Light Festivals, and otherwise entry is free. About fifty people are employed for the maintenance of the Great Garden under the direction of Dr Hans Preissel of the Herrenhausen Garden Administration. Ten extra labourers are taken on from the ranks of the unemployed, to help with weeding during the summer months. An extra technician is also employed to supplement the normal quota of four plumbers and electricians since, between May

49 Dolphin fountain by von Verschaffelt (1775) in one of the compartments in the bosquet at Schwetzingen

50 The Mosque at Schwetzingen designed by Nicholas de Pigage (1778–9)

and September, the gardens are illuminated and the fountains played four times a week in the evenings.

Description and history

The creation of the Great Garden was begun by Duke Johann Friedrich (1665–79) whose conversion of Herrenhausen into his summer residence was influenced by his visits to Venetian villas and their gardens. However, it was the Electress Sophie, wife of Ernst-August (1679–98), who, with the aid of the gardener Martin Charbonnier, gave the garden the form which, by and large, it has today. Shortly after her death in 1714, her son George succeeded to the British throne, and the subsequent absence of its owners ensured that the Baroque garden survived, almost unchanged, through the great landscaping fashions of the eighteenth century. The Baroque hedge theatre is one of the finest in Europe. The garden is bounded, Dutch-style, by canals and two pavilions by Remy de la Fosse, built in 1708–9, form the focal points of the lime avenues which border them. The oldest feature of the garden is the Grand Cascade built to an Italian design in 1676.

The restoration undertaken by the City Council in 1937 included various changes to the garden. The box pattern of the main parterre was replanted and filled with bedding plants, and a raised terrace was built to the west. The carp ponds behind the Grand Parterre were raised and enclosed in stone, and beyond them eight special gardens were laid out to demonstrate the development of garden design: Renaissance, Baroque and Rococo gardens, North German flower and rose gardens, a 'Bowling Green' garden, an Island garden and a Spring water garden. A maze was planted to a design by Perronet. The significance of Herrenhausen therefore lies not merely in its survival as one of the great Baroque gardens of Europe, but also in the changes wrought by the 1930s 'restoration'. Much of this was destroyed, together with the palace during the war but, in 1958 a seven-year plan was devised for a new phase of restoration completed in 1966.

Restoration and maintenance

The current care and maintenance of the garden has included the restoration of the 1930s North German rose garden, and experimental planting to devise a satisfactory plant mix for the parterres. Further historical research was initiated in 1989, and there is an intention to produce a management plan, but this will probably be put out to private tender. The administration would like to see the gradual restoration of

51 One of four, originally low-lying,
fishponds which were altered to stone-
lined basins with fountains in the 1930s

52 The North German rose garden

small areas of the garden to their seventeenth-century form. The triangular compartments of the bosquets, for instance, were once meadow grass with fruit trees, and one might be replanted to demonstrate the original concept. Totally exact historical reconstruction, however, is not considered necessary. Modern hybrids have been used in the restoration of the Rose Garden, and the development of a mixed planting for the parterres is concentrated on finding plants which are healthy, of a good colour and the right height, although research sources include *La Théorie et la Pratique du Jardinage* and the work documented in *Gartendenkmalpflege*.

Parterres

At present there are two plantings in the parterres, in May and October, and it is hoped that a satisfactory mix for spring planting will be developed in four or five years time. Unexpected hazards complicate the process; rabbits chewed holes in the 1989 experimental planting after finding the wallflowers a tasty addition to their diet. Winter bedding is still done in single colour masses of one species, viola, using a total of 130,000 plants. In 1988 the first mixed summer bedding was planted, 80,000 plants in eighteen different species. The planting is simplified by using an iron grid in a 1.8×2.7m wooden frame to aid spacing.

Hedges

Until recently the box hedges in the parterres at Herrenhausen presented a major maintenance problem. Since the plants were not hardy in Hanover's winter climate (which can be severe with temperatures falling twenty degrees below zero for prolonged periods) spruce boughs were used to protect the broderie in winter. This practice was time consuming and therefore discontinued in the late 1960s, and a hardy cultivar selected for planting from the surviving plants. Unfortunately the new cultivar was considered unsatisfactory, largely because its leaves discoloured in winter, so between 1972 and 1980 horticultural trials were carried out on thirty-four Buxus cultivars to find a better alternative. The result, *Buxus sempervirens* 'Blauer Heinz', not only retains its blue-green colour throughout winter but has also further reduced the maintenance burden as, owing to its upright growth form, it only requires clipping on the top once a year. Moreover the cuttings root easily although some browning of the leaves can take place during the first winter due to transplant shock.

The box hedges are cut by hand in May, and the clippings are collected using a suction cleaner. Hornbeam hedges are cut by machine in July or August, and the limes are pruned during the winter, usually in January and February. The smaller limes are pruned by hand from special scaffolding on rollers. The larger ones are cut, the sides only, every four years using motorised saws from a rented, hydraulic lift.

Weed and algae control

Herbicides can be applied between the box hedges in the parterres but their use is not permitted on the gravel paths. Machines for burning off weed growth have proved to be loud, expensive, and less effective than pedestrian wear, so a vibration machine is being tried. It both rakes and smooths, and has the added advantage that it helps drainage. Within the broderie plastic sheeting has been used under the gravel to suppress weed growth, but with poor results. Weeds, notably Schachtelhalm which can have a one and a half metre long root system, grow under the sheeting and emerge in the box hedges whence they are difficult to remove by hand. As it does not damage the box, Caseron G is applied at a rate of thirty kilos per hectare, but the combination of poor drainage and accumulated herbicides on the plastic sheeting encourages the growth of algae. The white gravel turns green and then presents a cleaning problem since it is difficult to replace, the source of supply being Italian through firms based in Frankfurt. In the orangery parterre, which was laid out to a chequered design in the 1960s, the Herrenhausen administration has been able to experiment with a new material, a perforated metal sheet with raised edges. This allows easy lifting of the gravel for cleaning and the washing of individual sheets. It also drains well, reduces weed growth and permits the application of herbicides or simple hand weeding. It is, however, new and more difficult to lay, and unfamiliar to the gardeners, who are not yet happy with it.

The water supply for the garden comes from the river via the canals. Clear mirror surfaces are important in the formal water basins and, until now, copper sulphate has been applied once a year to control algae, but work is being done to find an alternative.

Sculpture

The care and restoration of the stone sculptures during the 1960s included their repainting in dazzling white to imitate marble, a practice which had become unfashionable during the nineteenth century when the weathered face of the sandstone was preferred. The figures in the baroque theatre have also been re-gilded.

Avenues

The lime avenues flanking the canals currently present the greatest management problem. It is planned to fell and replant them in eight phases between 1992 and 2000, and the new plants are now being raised in the nursery. Fifteen years ago the main Herrenhausen avenue was replanted amid considerable opposition and a virulent newspaper campaign, which taught the administration the value of favourable publicity. It is hoped that it will be possible to harness the visible success of the first replanted avenue to belay any further opposition to what is an essential measure of good planting management.

Summer events

Approximately nine hundred trees are grown in vases and put outside at the end of April or beginning of May, and taken in again in September. A special greenhouse was erected for them in 1969 so that the old Orangery could be used for display purposes. The garden administration has a good relationship with the Department of Culture. Large events are held in the space once occupied by the palace, and both the Baroque and little theatres are used in July and August. In 1990 the triangular compartments of the bosquets were used for sound sculptures by a Swiss artist. Less satisfactory is the running of the congress centre and café, whose separate administration by the City causes some conflict with that of the garden.

Presentation

A stone plaque placed at the entrance to the garden in 1720 shows that the gardens were always accessible to the public. The conservation of the garden aims to balance its presentation and use as a public park with the recognition of its historic significance. Aesthetic qualities and high standards of horticultural maintenance have so far been considered more important than historic accuracy but, as modern techniques enable the cleaning of historic plant varieties and the successes of conservation projects elsewhere become more widely known perhaps the two will be better reconciled in future.

SCHLOSS AUGUSTUSBERG, BRÜHL

Location, ownership and management

The Schloss Augustusberg at Brühl, approximately halfway between Cologne and Bonn, is owned by the state of Nordrhein-Westfalen and its upkeep, together with that of the hunting lodge Schloss Falkenlust, is administered by the Schlossverwaltung Brühl under the municipal authority in Cologne. Responsibility for restoration measures lies with the Rheinisches Amt für Denkmalpflege, Bonn, under the directorship of Dr Wilfried Hansmann. The parterre and water garden was first restored in the 1930s and was the earliest garden restoration in Germany to be based on historic plans. Repairs were carried out in 1946 after the war, but by 1974 it was evident that the parterre garden needed further attention and a new restoration plan was initiated. Twenty-four gardeners are employed for the maintenance of the garden.

Description and history

The garden was designed by Dominique Girard and François Curvillié during the first half of the eighteenth century and altered, largely on the periphery, freeing the form of the boundary canal to incorporate an 'English garden' by P. J. Lenné, in the second half of the century. Early this century the parterres had vanished under grass, but the bordering lime allées survived. Between 1933 and 1935 the parterres were restored using Girard's plan dating from 1728 and the 1709 edition of Dézallier's *La Théorie et la Pratique du Jardinage* as references. In the 1960s a modern re-creation was carried out to the side of the main parterre garden, and the flanking fountain pools were reconstructed. The subsequent restoration, begun in 1974, was prompted by the bulging and cracking of the retaining borders and banks of the mirror pond, and by the loss of clarity in the parterre broderie.

Restoration

Water features

The restoration plan included the renewing of the basin of the great fountain, the mirror pond and the connecting cascade, the laying of electric cables, replacement of the water system and resurfacing of the garden terrace. The mirror pond was tackled first. It was drained and divested of a 25cm layer of silt. The southern edge and the entry to the cascade were rebuilt in reinforced concrete on a 50cm concrete foundation, and clad with basalt slabs using chromium nickel steel ties. The profile is simpler than the original stone but, by keeping the joints narrow and using a coloured mortar, the disparity in their appearance has been minimised. The porous gravel and sand base of the pool was compacted, raised 5cm by the addition of new material, and a new watertight lining (a 2cm fine asphalt and concrete mix) laid. A 3cm joint round the circumference was filled with a longlife mastic. A drain and pump were installed in the south-east corner for future maintenance, and finally the banks were re-turfed.

Parterres

It was at first intended to renew the parterres completely. Costs, however, would have been prohibitive, and the original restoration was found to be remarkably accurate, its outlines only obscured due to the coarsening of the arabesques through over or undercutting during routine maintenance, and because of the overmaturity of the box hedging which had died in places, so a decision was taken to revitalise the parterres using cuttings from the best plants. In 1980 30,000 boxwood (*Buxus arborescens*) cuttings were taken, and replanting was begun in 1981. Girard's 1728 plan showed only the green parts of the parterre and no planting plan or list survived for the plates-bandes. Reference was made to Girard's earlier plan for Schleissheim (1715–17), which follows the instructions given by Dézallier, in order to clarify the use of colour within the parterre. The contrasting red (brick dust) around the light green (grass) cordons de gazon had been omitted in the 1930s restoration and remains so. The Schleissheim plan shows no difference between the path and the background to the broderie and so white gravel has been used in these areas as a substitute for sand, but the arabesques are infilled with black, using basalt chips to replace the original coal dust.

In contrast to the Schleissheim plan, Girard's plan for Brühl shows no yew or ornamental trees within the parterre. By the late 1720s fashion had changed and these trees were left out, the corner accents being made by sculpture or vases on a pedestal. According to the eighteenth-century sovereign, Kurfurst Clemens August, the yew pyramids were substitutes for sculpture. They were planned for the corners only, but have proved difficult to grow. The arabesques at the end of the parterres are protected from trampling by a low metal railing which, like the raised concrete edging, is inevitably intrusive and not entirely successful.

Despite the lack of a historical reference for planting in the plates-bandes,

53 The parterres with the great fountain, cascade and mirror pond in the background

54 Parterre detail – the protective railing round the arabesques

55 One of the fountain pools reconstructed in the 1960s

the colour mix from the 1930s was close to the original concept. The shading on Girard's plan indicated a change in height from the centre to the edge of the beds. In the 1930s this was achieved by stacking the plants according to their height, but the centre line of the beds is now raised 15cm from the outer edge so that the soil profile is a hump-backed ridge. Only two plantings are currently carried out, and as yet the Schlossverwaltung has been unable to afford to change the early planting of mixed colour violas. Since 1984, however, a mixed summer planting based on the Grand Trianon plan of 1693 has been done. An early experimental planting showed that it took less time to plant this type of rhythmical, repeating pattern than to plant a modern mixed border. Each year 86,000 plants are grown in the nurseries for bedding out in the parterres.

'English garden'

A survey is presently being done on the remaining part of P. J. Lenné's English garden design with a view to extending the scope of the restoration. It is hoped to make use of plans and black and white photographs which are in the archives at Potsdam. This should be made much easier following the unification of East and West Germany in the autumn of 1990.

GIVERNY

Jardin palette ... d'un peintre fou de fleurs

Location, ownership and management

The garden at Giverny was the creation of the artist Claude Monet, and the subject of numerous of his paintings, from 1883 until the end of his life in 1926. The village of Giverny is situated in the Seine valley, about seventy kilometres north west of Paris. After Monet's death the garden was looked after by his daughter-in-law, Blanche. Between her death in 1940 and the death of Monet's second son, Michel, in 1966, care of the garden was gradually abandoned. When Michel died the property was left to the Académie des Beaux-Arts, and in 1977 Gerald van der Kemp was appointed 'Conservateur de Giverny' and began the rescue of the garden with the aid of the head gardener, M. Gilbert Vahé. The restoration of Giverny was made financially feasible through

56   The garden at Giverny depends for its effect on the quality of its planting

57   Visitors crowd the narrow paths

the work of two charitable foundations: La Société des Amis de Claude Monet, Giverny, and the Versailles Foundation, New York, and by the generosity of its patrons, principally Americans. Over the six months when the garden is open 250,000 visitors can be expected, not surprisingly, many of them American. Five full-time gardeners plus five seasonal workers are currently employed for the maintenance of the garden, but the initial restoration work was carried out by the three gardeners over the four years from 1977 to 1980.

Description

The garden depends for its effect on the quality of its planting and the combinations of flowers, which Monet used in a way that can best be compared to the selection of colours from a palette when painting. It defies the French gardening tradition, but is part of a wider movement towards the purer use of plants for their decorative form and colour, being comparable to the work of Gertrude Jekyll or that of Vita Sackville-West at Sissinghurst. Above all the garden is the result of the unique vision of a man who said of himself, 'En dehors de la peinture et du jardinage, je suis bon à rien!' It is undoubtedly the case that Monet's garden gives a great insight to his work as a painter and vice versa. The conservation of the garden has been largely dependent on the goodwill and interest of Americans. It is doubtful whether this would have been so readily forthcoming were it not for the association of garden and historic personality which lends itself to the American preservation ideal.

Restoration and maintenance

The restoration of the garden was based on research into the writings and recollections of visitors, photographs and Monet's paintings. New lines of research are always followed up in order to improve the accuracy of the planting. It is evident that much of the policy for the restoration has been influenced by the sheer number of visitors and their effective management within the confines of a private garden of moderate size. Donations enabled the provision of a car park on land behind the house and the building of an underground passageway to allow access from the house and flower garden to the water garden on the other side of the railway. Most of the gravel paths between the flower beds have been chained off so that the gardeners can continue weeding and maintenance work relatively unimpeded even when the garden is crowded. The paths which form the main pedestrian routes have been resurfaced in concrete, but using the same gravel as aggregate to match

58 Gardener and visitors in the water garden

59 Visitors include school groups

the other paths as closely as possible. By comparison, the brilliant green and white of the plastic chains make a mockery of such a careful choice of surface, and a more sympathetic material would reduce the visual intrusion.

Planting

For the herbaceous planting 5,000 flowers, annuals and perennials, are produced in the nursery each year. Herbicides are used on the gravel paths but, because of the nature of the planting, all other weeding is done by hand. The major obstacle to the successful growth and maintenance is the excessively calcareous nature of the soil which causes the yellowing of foliage. This problem has recently been tackled by the installation of a chemical plant to add nitrogen and phosphate to the watering system.

Visitors

M. Vahé considers that the worst problem posed by visitors to Giverny is their vociferous dislike of changes to the planting regardless of whether they are consistent with historic accuracy. Complaints from visitors are a thorn in the side of any hard-working gardener, especially when the restricted space makes contact between gardener and visitor unavoidable and the busy gardener an easy target for criticism. The guidebook is both informative and a colourful souvenir but, although credit is given for the garden's conservation, it concentrates on Monet himself and the history and descriptions of the garden. A section detailing the conservation measures and the approach taken to the planting might profitably be added to extend the visitor's perception.

DÉSERT DE RETZ

Mais n'est-ce pas déjà beau que d'une epoque on sauve un poème?
Colette

Location, ownership and management

The Désert de Retz borders the royal Forest of Marly near Chambourcy on the outskirts of Paris. It is owned by Jean-Marc Heftler and Olivier

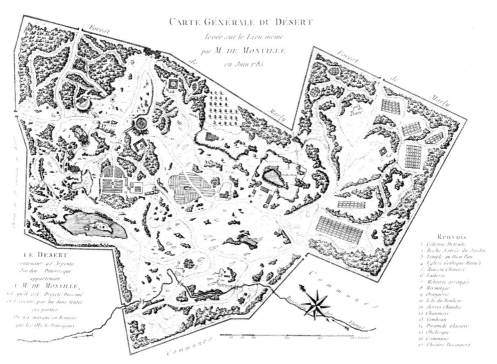

60   General plan of the Désert, 1785

61   View across the central valley to the ruined column

123

Choppin de Janvry who together formed the 'Société Civile du Désert de Retz' in 1984 for the purpose of rescuing and restoring the landscape and its garden buildings. They are supported by an association of friends, the 'Société des Amis du Désert de Retz'. The Désert was the creation of François de Monville in the fifteen years immediately preceding the French Revolution. There were originally twenty buildings set within the thirty-eight hectares of garden policies. Following the death of the then owner, Frédéric Passy, in 1936, attempts to initiate conservation measures were frustrated by the bureaucratic process, the reluctance of the state to take over and the refusal of the new owner to co-operate. Years of neglect led to the colonisation of the glades by ash and sycamore, the ruin of many of the buildings by falling trees or encroaching vegetation, and the final collapse of the Chinese house in 1970. Restoration is now in progress under the permanent supervision of M. Pierre Dupas. The cost of the first phase is estimated at 11,000,000 francs, of which fifty per cent will be met by the Ministère de la Culture et de la Communication. A second phase to provide visitor facilities and to reconstruct the demolished buildings will cost a further 13,000,000 francs. It is hoped that the Désert will be open to the public in 1993, but at present L'Association Histoire de Chambourcy, Retz et Aigremont organise visits on weekend afternoons and guided visits can be arranged by appointment.

Description and history

The Désert is a significant example of a 'jardin pittoresque' of which few survive in France owing to the greater interest in the grand 'jardin à la française', particularly after the Second World War. The eclectic range of buildings, dominated by the ruined column house, reflect the known world of the eighteenth century, a miniature earthly paradise entered, appropriately, through a grotto. The main entrance was placed on the forest boundary in order to attract the attention of the King. De Monville first lived in the Chinese house before the ruined column was built. It was a retreat within a retreat with its own water garden, and was probably the first attempt to construct a Chinese house in Europe. The ruined column, however, was the *pièce de résistance*, representing the crumbling of the ancient order and, through its curvilinear interior plan, the supremacy of the natural. The plan was copied by Thomas Jefferson in one of his early designs for the Capitol in Washington. From each bay of the column a different vista opens from the window to another garden building, the théâtre découvert, the Temple of Pan, the Chinese house, the pyramide glacière, the Gothic church. Only the obelisk stood at a distance. To Thomas Blaikie, working at the time for the Duke of Chartres, all was small, complicated and too near, but

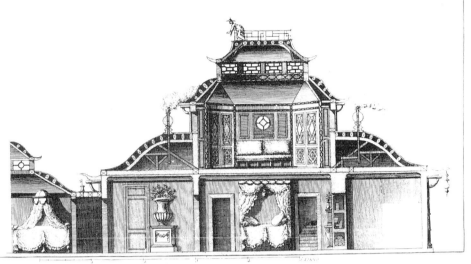

Coupe de la Maison Chinoise sur la Largeur en Face du Jardin

62 Section of the Chinese house

63 The ruined column in the process
of restoration (1988)

to numerous others, among them Jefferson, Gustav III of Sweden, and later, André Breton and the Surrealists, the writer Colette, and the dynamic Minister of Culture, André Malraux, it was an inspired landscape garden with a vital place in France's cultural heritage.

Although five of the Désert's buildings were proposed as 'Monuments Historiques' in 1937, a change of ownership delayed classification until 1941, by which time war had intervened. After the war a damning report by a government inspector, who found the Désert bizarre and less meritorious than other, grander schemes, consigned the Désert to oblivion for another twenty years until its cause was taken up by André Malraux. 'La Loi Malraux', which enables the state to initiate repairs to a classified monument and to require from the owner up to fifty per cent of the costs, was passed in 1966. The relevant decree for the Désert was authorised in 1971 and notified to the proprietor the following year. In the absence of any response, work finally commenced in 1973. Between 1973 and 1979 essential repairs were made to some of the buildings, panels from the Chinese house were recovered and preserved, and the surviving elements and the known documentary evidence were faithfully recorded, but, except for the removal of fallen trees from the paths and buildings and the stripping of creepers from the column, no attempt was made to treat the planted elements. The odds against the upkeep of the Désert were enormous. Work could only be done during six months of the year and, in the intervening periods all was left to go to rack and ruin as before. The owner refused to make any financial contribution or to talk either of restoration or of selling, and the state hesitated. The impasse was finally resolved when the Groupe Worms bought the Société Fermière et de Participations and with it, its assets at the end of 1981. In 1984 it ceded ownership to the Société Civile du Désert de Retz. At the end of 1987 the National Assembly voted to retain the Désert as an area for priority action under the historic monuments programme and agreed in principle to state funding for a further five years starting from New Year 1988.

Restoration

Research and planning

A wealth of documentation on the Désert has been collated thanks to the efforts of the two proprietors and of Pierre-Emile Renard, president of L'Association Histoire de Chambourcy, Retz et Aigremont, and a study detailing the history of the Désert and the intentions of the Société Civile for its future has been drawn up by M. Choppin de Janvry. The restoration scheme is based on plans dating from 1785, 1811 and 1842,

64 Olivier Choppin de Janvry and Pierre Dupas discuss the significance of the pyramide glacière with student visitors

65 The newly reconstructed tente tartare on the Isle du Bonheur

a survey and photographs taken since 1850, and a recent inventory of the oldest trees. Some plants were conserved in the National Museum during the Revolution and lists exist for the glasshouses and the orangery. There are numerous engravings and drawings, some of which are preserved in the museum of the Ile-de-France and in private collections.

The 1811 plan is being used as a guide for the restoration of the central valley as it is easier to read the massing of de Monville's planting in the semi-mature trees recorded on it. A comparison between this plan and a plan of the trees in the recent inventory shows that an intelligent programme of replanting, respecting the main vista, was carried out by Frédéric Passy during the second half of the nineteenth century. Twenty hectares of the landscape park were put into cultivation after the Revolution and had therefore changed out of all recognition by 1811. The restoration of these areas will be based on the 1785 plan.

Problems and progress

Clearing of the vegetation to re-open the vistas is now largely complete, some donated trees have been planted, and a new 'tente tartare' has been erected on its island site. It was decided to concentrate building efforts on the ruined column and, for security reasons, to create a residential apartment on the second floor. The internal partitions are being rebuilt from records made in 1963 and 1973 and an analysis of photographs. The proprietors would like to see the Désert become an interdisciplinary centre for the study of historic parks and gardens which would be housed on the ground and first floors.

The chief remaining problem is one of access and security. Historically, access through the Royal Forest to the Désert was granted by the King, and the inhabitants had a right to a 'tour d'échelle', a twelve-foot wide path around the outside of the boundary wall. The Forest Office has unilaterally withdrawn this right but, ironically, since the forest is now open to the public and the Forest Office has failed to maintain the boundary wall, there is now free access through breaches where the stone has crumbled. Negotiations continue with the Forest Office to ensure the upkeep of the wall and the restitution of the right of access, but plans are afoot to secure the restoration of the wall and of the twenty hectares put under cultivation during the Revolution in return for the lease of the surrounding fields as a golf course, which will be built without the visual scars of bunkers on the historic landscape.

PAINSHILL PARK

Location, ownership and management

Painshill Park lies in the borough of Elmbridge, just west of Cobham, Surrey in the south of England. The Hon. Charles Hamilton designed and laid out the pleasure grounds and surrounding park between 1738 and 1773, gradually increasing the size of the estate to over one hundred hectares. When Hamilton sold the estate it became the property of a succession of appreciative owners until 1948 when it was bought by a speculator. Part of it had been sold in separate lots before a local pressure group persuaded Elmbridge Borough Council to buy the remaining sixty-four hectares between 1974 and 1980 for a total cost of £195,000, to which both Surrey County Council and the Countryside Commission contributed. Painshill is leased to the Painshill Park Trust, formed in 1981 to restore the park and open it to the public.

The Trust employs a small team of permanent staff under the direction of Janie Burford, a landscape architect. Much of the labour has been supplied by the Manpower Services Commission (prior to September 1988), students from Merrist Wood Agricultural College, the British Trust for Conservation Volunteers and other volunteers. Contractors are used for specialist operations and consultants are employed where appropriate. In 1984 Land Use Consultants (LUC) produced a master plan for the restoration. The plan was funded by the National Heritage Memorial Fund which also granted a sum of £1,000,000 for restoration work over the three years between 1985 and 1987. The Countryside Commission and the Historic Buildings and Monuments Commission have given grant aid on a percentage basis. Other donations have come from Surrey County Council, grant-making trusts, companies and individual donors. The master plan envisaged the completion of much of the capital works within ten years, and the remainder after a further fifteen years, the total cost amounting to several million pounds.

Description and history

Like so many eighteenth-century gardens, Painshill was the work of a dedicated amateur. The youngest son of the Earl of Abercorn, Hamilton was a painter, collector and plantsman who had travelled widely and turned to landscape design to fulfil his creative aspirations. Unfortunately his efforts left him impoverished and he was forced to sell, but the park was much visited and justly renowned during the latter half of the eighteenth century. It was praised by Walpole, sketched by William

Gilpin, and featured on the Imperial Russian dinner service commissioned from Josiah Wedgwood in 1773. The design centred on the lake, an extensive 5.6 hectare stretch of water complete with islands, grotto and Chinese bridge. The water supply was fed through a cascade by a water wheel on the River Mole which runs, at a lower level, along the southern boundary of the park. A perambulation of the pleasure grounds took the visitor through a series of pictorial scenes planted both to contrive the best views and to reinforce the atmosphere evoked by a particular garden building. A cathedral of trees reflected in nature the ogee arches of the Gothic temple, yews reinforced the sombre mood of the mausoleum, and pines enhanced the savage wilderness of the steep woods around the hermitage in a manner reminiscent of the landscape paintings of Salvator Rosa. It seems likely that Hamilton deliberately chose Painshill for the natural attributes of the site. The variations in landform afforded by its position on the north side of the river contributed much to the quality of the design, especially of the ornamental grounds. To the north a crescent of open parkland, planted by Hamilton with clumps of trees, foreshadowed the future development of the landscape park in England. The present boundaries of the site preclude the house and most of the parkland to the north. After more than thirty years of neglect, in 1981 Painshill was an almost impenetrable jungle of vegetation, the lake was silted and stagnant, some of the garden buildings had disappeared, and most of those surviving were in need of urgent repair. After much clearance work and replanting, further havoc was wreaked by the storm in October 1987 when a thousand trees were lost.

Restoration

The policy for the park as stated by its owner, Elmbridge Borough Council, is,

> that Painshill Park and the Follies be restored as nearly as possible to Charles Hamilton's original design and concept of a landscape garden with a variety of scenery, for the benefit of the public and with the aim of making the Park a self-supporting enterprise.

The work of the Trust at Painshill has been based on a considerable archive of documents and photographs collated by the archivist, Mavis Collier. After the initial heavy work, eighteenth-century techniques will be used as far as possible for the park's maintenance. The restoration is perhaps most notable for the use of archaeological investigations and the restoration of eighteenth-century planting, and most notorious for the extended planning dispute over the siting of the car park. Planning

66   The Chinese bridge and replanted peninsula

permission for the car park was granted to the Trust on appeal to the Secretary of State. However, the Trust was prevented from implementing the scheme by the two landowners involved, one of them Elmbridge Borough Council itself, who, having offered the land for the car park, then withdrew the offer after planning permission had been won. Negotiations for another site are now taking place and it is hoped that this time the Trust will be successful, enabling the Park to open fully in two or three years' time.

Progress

A considerable achievement of restoration targets is already obvious to visitors who are shown round during the, at present limited, opening times by excellent volunteer guides. The lake has been dredged, its edge re-formed, and the cascade, aqueduct and water wheel restored. Many of the paths and lawn areas and the tiled floor of the mausoleum have been re-laid. The Gothic temple and the Chinese bridge have been restored, and the abbey repainted. The foundations of the grotto were consolidated whilst the water level in the lake was low, and work continues on the interior. The Gothic tower has now been restored with two floors converted to provide accommodation for a warden, leaving the ground and top floors and roof level viewing platform accessible to visitors. The replanting of the amphitheatre and the Chinese bridge peninsula to designs researched by Mark Laird has been completed, and a blueprint for the rest of the replanting should be ready by the end of 1990.

Planting

The layout of the evergreen amphitheatre was based on a plan by John Roque drawn in 1744. The Roque plan was not a detailed planting plan, and research was necessary to establish what plants were available to Hamilton, their likely disposition and their current availability before replanting was feasible. Of the thirty species of holly, for example, which Hamilton might have used, only nine are still in cultivation. Hamilton's correspondence with his suppliers was cross-checked with eighteenth-century reference books such as Philip Miller's *Gardeners' Dictionary* of which Hamilton was known to have a copy. Nursery catalogues were searched for the one hundred and seventy-seven species of the plants required. Twenty-two of the total were unavailable commercially and had to be grown from cuttings. A contemporary plan by Lord Petre, dated 1737/8, of a similar evergreen plantation for the Duke of Norfolk at Worksop was used as a guide to the planting

67 The stark image of the Gothic abbey reflected in the lake

68 Green oak laths support the gypsum flakes of the stalactiform projections in the grotto

pattern and spacing. A small area was planted as a test plot in spring 1986 before full planting was begun in the autumn.

On the Chinese bridge peninsula a description of the walks and planting written by Sir John Parnell in 1763 was confirmed by the discovery of a path network during the historic tree survey in 1982, and by further archaeological investigation in 1986 when the paths were found to be broad walks which were most probably grassed. In the absence of any planting plan, the design of this area has been based on contemporary books, descriptions and illustrations, including a 1760 engraving. Seventy of the two hundred and seventy species required were not available from commercial sources when planting began in autumn, 1987, and spring, 1988, but the gaps will be filled as the plants are found.

Archaeology

Archaeological investigation has played a considerable part in the research and survey work at Painshill. The remains of Hamilton's brick and tile kilns were excavated under the floor of the ruined abbey. Plaster was found at the site of the Temple of Bacchus, proving that it was of timber construction, and the foundations of the Turkish tent were located by using the resistivity test developed by Drs Martin and Clark of the University of Surrey.[1]

Construction techniques

Some lessons have been learned about the use of modern techniques in reconstructing historic designs. The painting of the abbey seems too stark, although it is an accurate interpretation from an eighteenth-century painting which shows it starkly white. While it is hoped that it will eventually be adequately disguised by creepers, it is now thought that painting with the original limewash would have been better. In the grotto the stainless steel mesh, used in a first attempt to reconstruct the stalactiform projections from the roof, was insufficiently rigid to support the surface finish of gypsum flakes, and so the original method of construction, using a frame of green oak laths, was copied instead.

Publicity

The Trust has always looked to the future of Painshill and recognised the essential role of publicity, education and the provision of facilities in achieving a state of financial self-sufficiency. Some of the publicity has been inadvertent, such as that surrounding the prolonged planning dispute over the car park, but most of it was the result of deliberate policies. Press releases are prepared every three or four weeks and in 1985 a National Press day was held. Peter Palumbo was appointed appeal chairman in 1987. A royal visit has been arranged for the opening of each building and HRH the Prince of Wales is now royal patron of the Trust. A group of volunteers, known as the Painshill ambassadors, give lectures wherever and whenever possible, and three videos, on the history, archaeology and planting of the park, are available for hire. The video on planting is particularly well done and of interest to all ages.

Education

Painshill has played a part in training programmes through the MSC schemes and the provision of practical experience for students at Merrist Wood. A schools education programme was started in 1983/4 and there is now a classroom and a full-time teacher supplied by Surrey County Council. A very successful summer camp was run by the Trust staff in 1989.[2]

Visitors

Better facilities are needed for greater numbers of visitors, and are planned in the area around the walled garden. Schemes are being devised for selling goods in the visitors' shop. At present there is Painshill honey, and Painshill wine may be available after the restoration of the vineyard. The introduction of Jacob sheep and the use of the park by the Sussex Working Horse Trust are other activities planned in keeping with the intention to use eighteenth-century maintenance techniques.

At present approximately 250 visitors can be expected on each of the twenty-six afternoons that Painshill is open, and another 100 come on pre-booked tours during the week. Anyone considering the provision of guided tours in a historic garden would do well to accompany one of the Painshill guides on a walk round the park to learn what the experience can offer. The guides are extremely well-versed in their subject, gear their observations to the interests of the individuals in their group, and above all succeed in making Painshill come alive. The printed guide to Painshill is also to be commended for its sensible use of heavy card which makes it easy to handle even in windy weather. Unfortunately it is anticipated that it will prove too expensive to reprint on the same quality of paper.

BIDDULPH GRANGE GARDENS

Location, ownership and management

The Biddulph Grange estate covered some forty hectares of swampy and hilly ground in Staffordshire, England, three miles south of Congleton. The gardens were the work of Mr James Bateman, a noted collector and a specialist on orchids, and his wife, Maria, during the 1840s and 1850s, with the help and advice, particularly on the design of the built features, of Edward Cooke, a landscape painter. Biddulph Grange itself is now an orthopaedic hospital administered by the North Staffordshire Hospital Management Committee. In 1988, after a long history of concern for the survival and maintenance of the gardens, six hectares were acquired by the National Trust from the Staffordshire Moorlands District Council who made a successful bid to take over the estate from the area health authority. Although most of the original gardens remained, the terraces had been altered to make way for extensions to the hospital, the condition of some of the buildings was unsafe and aggravated by vandalism, and the planting was very overgrown. At present the head gardener is assisted by four gardeners and two trainees, one on the government's Youth Training Scheme and the other sponsored by the Stanley Smith Horticultural Trust. The garden was bought for £50,000 and, in contrast to the National Trust's usual policy, without an endowment. The National Heritage Memorial Fund has contributed £300,000 to the project, and forty per cent of the building costs, including the restoration of all built structures down to steps and path edgings, has been obtained in grant aid from English Heritage. An application was also made to the special fund administered by the EEC Department of Culture. The Trust has launched an appeal to raise £800,000 to meet the remaining costs of restoration. The garden opened in May 1991, but prior to the official opening guided tours took place on request.

Description

The imprint of Victorian gardeners survives in many present-day gardens and parks, but there are few which give so complete a picture of Victorian gloom and grandeur, eclectic design and mania for plants as Biddulph Grange. Only the dahlia walk had been filled in, and the parterres lost in the alterations to the terraces in front of the house, when the need for positive action began to be fully appreciated in the 1970s. The rhododendron garden round the lake with its mirrored vista back to the house, the Egyptian garden with its doorway curiously

69 The Egyptian garden with one of the yew obelisks cut back to the trunk

70 Behind the doorway in the Egyptian garden – a half-timbered Cheshire summerhouse

leading to a half-timbered Cheshire summerhouse, the Chinese garden, the Wellingtonia avenue with its path designed to give the optical illusion of an obelisk, the Pinetum, and the lime walk were all intact. Bateman must have been conversant with Sir William Chambers' 'Dissertation on Oriental gardening'. The design of the 'Chinese garden' represents the zenith of interest in the Chinese landscape gardening style. Like the vanished house and garden of the Désert de Retz it is an isolated garden within a garden, but at Biddulph an attention to detail typical of the later period ensures that its isolation is more complete. The approach, through a rare example of a root tunnel or stumpery, gives entry to a remote and separate world, a fragment of 'China' planted with Chinese species, and hidden by the piled rocks of the 'Great Wall' which recall both the fascination with rockwork and the symbolism of the true Chinese garden. Bateman also had an orangery, a rhododendron and fern house, a separate camellia house, and an ornamental orchard where the trees were surrounded by clipped cotoneaster. The old gardens of his former residence, Knypersley Hall, became the fruit and vegetable gardens. The fact that in 1860 forty gardeners were employed at Biddulph gives some idea of the meticulous standard of maintenance and serves to emphasise the difficulties facing the National Trust in contemplating its upkeep today.

History

The ownership of Biddulph passed from James Bateman to the Heath family, father and son, before it was acquired as a hospital in 1926. In the early 1970s the interest of members of Tatton Garden Society and the Garden History Society prompted a report on the history and significance of the site by D. Baldwin of Manchester University which recommended that listed buildings procedure (under the Town and Country Planning Act of 1971) be undertaken for the buildings and their related features, and that a plan be drawn up for the restoration of the garden within the framework of a long-term maintenance programme. The Hospital Management Committee, realising the magnitude of the maintenance problem, approached the Royal Botanical and Horticultural Society of Manchester and the Northern Counties who sponsored a survey by Dr Mark Smith of the Bristol University Botanic Garden. By 1976 the health authority had decided that it would be unable to fund a restoration scheme, and wrote to the Garden History Society for help. They recommended that, since listed building status had been achieved for all the built structures in April 1974, a formal application for grant aid should be made to the Historic Buildings Council under Clause 12 of the Town and Country Amenities Act 1974, which made provision for historic gardens. A steering group was formed in 1976 with the aim of leasing and restoring the garden but negotiations with the health authority proved fruitless. Considerable publicity campaigning for the recognition of the garden's importance, including articles, television programmes and its illustration on a postage stamp, was eventually officially endorsed by its inclusion at Grade One status in the HBMC Register of Parks and Gardens and encouraged its acquisition by the National Trust.

Restoration

Research and planning

A tree and shrub survey and a report by Michael Lear based on historical research were prepared for the National Trust in 1987 before the Gardens became the property of the Trust. The main research material was a fulsome series of seven articles in the *Gardener's Chronicle* in 1857 and 1862, the original of the plan by E. Kemp which accompanied them, old photographs and subsequent articles. An archive is being kept for Biddulph using a card index system. The garden buildings were in a state of repair sufficient for their original form to be self evident and thus to enable authentic restoration, but English Heritage insisted on a major archaeological dig to determine the features of the dahlia walk and the parterres before restoration. Most of the structural work, apart from the parterre, will be finished before the opening date. The National Trust base their restoration work and subsequent maintenance on a policy statement, drawn up on the basis of the report and survey, rather than on a definitive management plan. The programme of work for the next six months is written in a report agreed at a site meeting between the head gardener, the gardens adviser, the manager or land agent and the historic buildings representative. In the case of Biddulph Grange both the latter posts are held by Julian Gibbs. All the planting is done by the property's gardening team, but architects were appointed for the restoration of the buildings and the work carried out by a main contractor with specialist sub-contractors. The restoration of freestanding ornaments was the responsibility of the Trust's own statuary workshop at Cliveden with the help of specialist craftsmen.

Problems and conflicts

The restoration at Biddulph has posed an interesting set of problems in its pursuit of authenticity, especially where visitors and the treatment of planting are concerned. The darkness of the tunnel and the grotto under the Chinese temple has necessitated a compromise between safety and historic accuracy in the provision of electric lighting. Modern techniques have been employed in the rebuilding of the rockwork using flexible stainless steel Spiro ties, instead of mortar, to keep the appearance naturalistic. In a garden where the plant collection plays a major part the business of labelling is vexing. Pottery, Victorian-style labels with the old names above and the modern botanical ones below are being considered. Unfortunately, labels, like plants, often prove tempting to visitors and using good ones could prove to be a costly exercise without adequate supervision. Since each part of the garden is hidden from the others, it has been decided to have volunteer 'room-watchers' supervising each area just as they do in National Trust houses. Luckily, each small garden can be watched from a garden building so these volunteers should not suffer too much in inclement weather! Volunteers have also been used for archaeological work rather than introduce an MSC team, and this has served to foster local interest. Access and car parking are problems which are not helped by the sharing of the site with the hospital. Temporary provision for cars has been made in the stable yard, which enables visitors to start a tour of the garden from the original waiting room which was built near the gardener's cottage, but it may prove necessary to use the back entrance to the garden at the end of the lime walk. The hospital extension to the old house is an eyesore from the terrace, though happily not from the lower level of the dahlia walk, and requires a departure from Bateman's design so that it can be screened off by planting.

Planting

The first planting problem was the cutting back of evergreens to allow sufficient light for replanting. Four years ago 1,000 yew trees were container grown for planting to repair the thirteen miles of hedging. Bateman favoured a wider spacing of the plants than is normal so that the restoration of the hedges is difficult. If they are cut back or replanted at the same spacing growth is slow so that the hedge remains gappy. It has to be decided whether this is acceptable or whether the spacing should be reduced. The yew obelisks in the Egyptian Court were severely cut back in order to restore their shape, but so far only one shows signs of regrowth so it may be necessary to replace both. The *Sequoia* in 'China' had grown so large as to be out of scale with the design of the garden. Because of the restrictions imposed by a Tree Preservation Order, the *Sequoia* has been cut and a new leader selected and trained rather than resort to removing the tree and replanting. The right varieties are hard to find for the replanting of the dahlia walk. Few nineteenth-century varieties now exist because disease destroyed so many at the end of the century. It has therefore been decided to plant comparable

71   The dahlia walk in the process of restoration

types. However, the dahlia walk was sunken, with hedges planted on top of the retaining walls allowing little sun to penetrate, and it remains to be seen whether it will be possible to sustain the growth of a reasonable number of dahlias in these conditions.

Information and publicity

The National Trust has the use of one of the main rooms of the house in which it will display an exhibition on the story of the restoration. It promises to be an interesting exercise. A film, financed in a fifty–fifty partnership with an independent company has been produced for sale nationally as a forty-minute video, and for archival purposes. The Trust have also published a book on the gardens by Peter Hayden.

MONTICELLO

And our own dear Monticello, where has nature spread so rich a mantle under the eye?

Jefferson

Location, ownership and management

Monticello, home of the American president (1801–9) Thomas Jefferson, was built on a small hill commanding a view over open countryside near Charlottesville, Virginia. Work on the site began in 1768, and both house and grounds were laid out to Jefferson's own design. The five thousand acre plantation is now owned by the Thomas Jefferson Memorial Foundation, a private non-profit-making organisation formed in 1923 to buy, restore and maintain Monticello as a national memorial to Jefferson. The Garden Club of Virginia was involved in the restoration of the flower garden between 1939 and 1941, but in the 1970s it was decided to embark on a restoration programme for the whole of the grounds. William Weistander, an architectural historian, has overall responsibility for the restoration plan and in 1977 Peter Hatch was appointed Director of Grounds and Gardens with responsibility also for horticultural research. Four full-time gardeners and eleven ground staff are employed, with students taken on as additional labour during the summer. A further three full-time staff are employed in the Thomas Jefferson Center for Historic Plants which opened in 1983. Monticello entertains 550,000 visitors each year, a fifth of whom also visit the exhibition centre, some two miles distant. In 1988 25,000 people were taken on garden tours for which ten part-time guides are employed.

Description and history

Although Jefferson studied law at Williamsburg and thereafter played a prominent part in the political life of America, he was also a proficient surveyor, taught by his father, and put this skill to use in his designs for the layout of the city of Washington and the University of Virginia at Charlottesville. While based in Paris as Minister to France, Jefferson travelled to Italy, the Low Countries, Germany and England, extending his knowledge of building and garden design, so that on his return to America he was frequently consulted on landscape and architectural matters by his contemporaries. He designed several plantations besides Monticello, where his admiration for the natural style of landscape gardening, and his belief that beauty and use were of equal importance in the laying out of grounds, were both demonstrated. Many of Jefferson's ideas were gleaned from books such as Shenstone's *Works* and Thomas Whately's *Observations on Modern Gardening*, and the influence of the English landscape style can be seen in his description for the planting of open groves of trees at Monticello which

> must be broken by clumps of thickets as the open grounds of the English are broken by clumps of trees.

Monticello was a veritable 'ferme ornée'. Above all, Jefferson was a gardener and delighted in new plants and in flowers. Of fruit trees alone he grew a total of one hundred and fifty different varieties of peaches, apples, cherries, pears, plums, apricots, almonds, nectarines, quinces, and walnuts. Many eighteenth-century plant discoveries were forwarded to Jefferson from the Jardin des Plantes in Paris, but nearly half of the flowers he grew were indigenous North American species. To cultivate his flowers he laid out a serpentine path, bordered by narrow beds, around the lawn in front of the house in 1807 and 1808 in addition to twenty oval beds within the four angles of the house. The vegetable garden was laid out on a terrace, 80 feet wide by 1,000 feet long, to the south of the house, and was used as an experimental plot for numerous different varieties, often displayed in an ornamental fashion. It was here, on top of the retaining wall, that Jefferson built his garden pavilion which became for him a favourite place to read. The orchard and garden at Monticello represented, in Peter Hatch's words, 'the state of the art of fruit and vegetable culture in the early 1800's'.

Restoration

Such was the design of Monticello, its horticultural interest, the intentions, landscape skills, knowledge and public standing of its owner and creator, Thomas Jefferson, that the estate has great significance in each category of the criteria specified as prerequisite for inclusion in the National Register of Historic Places. In recent times, the use of archaeological techniques in the investigation and restoration of the landscape, and the application of historic horticultural research have added to the significance of the site. A full understanding of the problems which beset garden conservation and the ways in which restoration can be achieved is difficult to envisage without reference to the work done at Monticello. In some respects the problem of restoration at Monticello has been simplified, compared to other landscapes with a long history of design and redesign, by the decision to restore the plantation to its appearance between 1809 and 1812 when Jefferson had just retired from the presidency and was at his most active at Monticello. Jefferson's own detailed notes and observations in his *Garden Book*, his drawings and correspondence, have formed the basis for the restoration. In 1979 the commitment to historic accuracy was marked by the start of a programme of archaeological investigation under the leadership of William Kelso, funded by the Thomas Jefferson Memorial Foundation and by grants from the National Endowment for the Humanities.

Archaeology

Excavations in the vegetable garden uncovered the remains of the stone terrace wall (subsequently rebuilt under the supervision of Rudi Favretti) and the foundation of the garden pavilion (reconstructed in 1984), and located the gateways from which the alignment of the twenty-four 'squares' or plots and the paths was determined. The investigation of post holes to find the position of Jefferson's ten foot high paling fence, of tree holes to confirm an 1812 orchard planting plan, and of stake holes in the vineyard, have also been part of the archaeological work. The slight discolouration of the soil which signifies post or planting holes was at first difficult to detect in the red clay soil at Monticello. The posts, however, were wedged with stones which, together with fragments of the original posts, were easier to find. Careful examination then revealed faint colour and textural differences in the soil. Armed with this experience, as well as a planting plan, it was easier to detect the soil stains of the tree holes in the orchard. Test trenches were dug to remove the ploughed depth of the soil. In the last cut, two- to three-foot diameter soil stains were found at twenty-five-foot centres running north west–south east across the south west facing slope. A cut made

72   The house at Monticello with its lawn and serpentine walk bordered by flowers

73   Part of the 1,000 foot long terrace of the vegetable garden

at right angles showed further stains at forty-five foot centres, thus confirming the layout shown on the plan. Excavations have also uncovered the back-filled ditch of what was once a type of ha-ha, known from contemporary descriptions to have been bridged by a horizontal fence which must have acted like a cattle grid.

The use of archaeology can itself cause frustration and further obstacles within the restoration process. The replanting of the orchard to the 1812 plan was delayed until the exact planting positions for the trees were ascertained by the archaeologists. Clumps of trees are known to have stood at the corners of the house. They have not been replanted despite the fact that the species of the trees and the boundaries of the planting areas are known, because the actual planting spot of each tree cannot be established (two of Jefferson's tulip trees are still standing) and planting might remove archaeological evidence. Although the line of the paling fence has now been determined there has been considerable opposition to its replacement because it would interrupt the view. The eastern white-tail deer, which the fence as designed to keep out, is still a pest which has required the placing of protective chicken-wire cages around all the orchard trees, so in this case it seems clear that practical necessity should combine with historic accuracy to overrule considerations of aesthetics. At the end of 1989 a temporary compromise was reached with the erection of the first one hundred-foot section of the fence.

Planting and maintenance

The restoration of the vineyard was also completed in 1989. Jefferson himself never successfully grew vines. His many attempts were doomed to failure because of the susceptibility of the European vine to disease and insect attack. In order to ensure that the restored vineyard should flourish, European vines have been grafted on to American rootstock in another compromise with historic accuracy. One of the greatest problems in the restoration of historic plantings is to trace and identify varieties of plants which are obscured by inconsistent nomenclature. Jefferson often described a plant by the name of the person or place whence it came, e.g. 'Taliferro apple', 'Tuscan bean', and plants have frequently had to be identified by comparison between descriptions and contemporary paintings. Few fruit trees come true from seed, so every new seedling is potentially a new variety which can only be reproduced by grafting. One of the first horticultural developments of eighteenth-century America was the production of new seedling apples. Jefferson grew at least eighteen varieties of apple and his 'Taliferro apple' has yet to be rediscovered. Even when historic varieties are rediscovered there are other hazards to their successful cultivation. Seeds of the Tennis-ball lettuce were obtained from the National Seed Storage laboratory and carefully nurtured in the Monticello vegetable garden. The garden produce is distributed amongst the employees at Monticello and, when word got out that Tennis-ball lettuce was the best ever tasted, all the lettuces were rapidly harvested, leaving none to go to seed for the following year. It was three years before Peter Hatch ventured to ask for a further supply of seed.

The vegetable garden today is an interpretation of the garden as it existed between 1807 and 1814, but with certain limitations. The garden is planted more intensively than in Jefferson's day, both to facilitate the collection of seed and to show more to the visitor. Where it has not been possible to trace the vegetable varieties actually grown by Jefferson, other nineteenth-century varieties have been substituted. For maintenance reasons the rows of vegetables are more widely spaced. Although nineteenth-century techniques are used where possible – peas are staked with brushwood, perennial vegetables are manured and, in the vineyard, the vines are tied with the silky thread from yucca leaves – modern tools such as rotovators are used to ease the maintenance burden. Because many old varieties of vegetables have been neglected due to the development of new, 'improved' varieties or have disappeared through their susceptibility to pests and diseases, modern technology, in the form of organic fertilisers, natural pesticides and irrigation, is employed at Monticello to preserve the diversity of the collection.

Information and presentation

Careful attention has been paid to labelling. In the flower garden where the borders along the winding walk are divided into ten-foot sections, each planted with a different flower, wooden labels with the common name writ large by hand and the botanical name, smaller, underneath have been used. Leaflets on both the vegetable and flower gardens have been printed. They are very informative and particularly interesting because they make clear the differences between the historic and the modern garden. In the vegetable garden 25,000 copies of the leaflets are available from discreetly placed boxes each year. The cost for two years' supply is five thousand dollars. The Thomas Jefferson Center for Historic Plants is extending Monticello's work on the conservation of plants by distributing plants and seeds for sale. Each plant sold is accompanied by a brief written history. The Center also promotes an educational programme which includes display gardens, lectures, information sheets and educational publications.

Visitor facilities

The Thomas Jefferson Center for Historic Plants lies some distance away from the house on a separate part of the estate, but there is a plant shop under canvas in the visitors' car park. The car park is located near to the access point from the road. Tickets are sold from a building in the car park and shuttle buses transport visitors to the house and garden, making the circuit back to the car park on a one-way system so that the approach is not marred or obstructed by endless visitor traffic. Visitors are also asked to confine picnicking to the area provided near the car park. Other visitor facilities include two gift shops, one above the vegetable garden, and the other at the exhibition centre on the main highway where there is a good, permanent display relating to Jefferson's life at Monticello.

BILTMORE ESTATE

Location, ownership and management

Biltmore Estate, home of the Vanderbilt family since the 1880s, lies near Asheville, North Carolina. George Vanderbilt gradually accumulated 125,000 acres of the French Broad River Valley and the Blue Ridge Mountain Range, much of it in small parcels of land which had been used for subsistence farming, and engaged Richard Morris Hunt and Frederick Law Olmsted to design the house and landscape respectively, creating an American version of one of the great European, working country estates. The house was inspired by the French châteaux of the Loire valley and French, Italian and English influences are evident in the grounds. The greater part of the estate was bequeathed to the nation after Vanderbilt's death, and now forms part of the Pisgah National Forest. Other land was sold for the development of the town of Biltmore Forest and the Blue Ridge highway, and two interstate highways have further encroached upon the estate, one crossing the park on a flyover, the other on the periphery. The remaining 12,500 acres were divided between Vanderbilt's two Cecil grandsons, and the house and gardens are part of the present, eight thousand acre, estate which has been open to the public since 1930. Visitor numbers have increased, particularly over the last ten years, and the annual total is now over 600,000. The landscape manager has a team of thirty ground staff for the maintenance of the policies.

Description and history

Biltmore is unusual in the context of the American conservation movement in that it is not the home of a historic personality. The house is a fulsome example of what wealth could achieve in terms of furnishing, works of art, comfort and modern conveniences in the home of one of the richest families in America at the turn of the century. The design of the grounds, however, derives much of its significance from being the last work of Frederick Law Olmsted, whose importance as a landscape architect has prompted the 'Olmsted Historic Landscape Preservation Program' in Massachusetts, and a nationwide movement for the legislative protection of his landscape parks. The significance of the Biltmore landscape was further enhanced by Olmsted's own insistence that the Vanderbilts employ a forester to manage the forestry resources of the estate, which had been eroded and impoverished by years of subsistence farming and the cutting and burning of woodland for grazing. The resulting management plan pioneered large-scale forestry management in America. Its author, George Pinchot, went on to help found the US Forestry Service, and his successor at Biltmore started the first American school of forestry.

Olmsted's concept for the design of the landscape encompassed the laying out of formal gardens and pleasure grounds next to the house, surrounded by a two hundred and fifty acre deer park. He proposed the farming, mainly for livestock, of the land in the river bottom, and the reafforestation of the rest of the estate for a commercial timber crop. The 'rampe douce' facing the house is deliberately reminiscent of Vaux-le-Vicomte. On the south, below the terraced, Italian garden, is a large shrub garden or 'ramble' which leads to a four-acre walled garden and the conservatory and greenhouses. His design of the park with its bass pond, lake and groups of trees, is open and pastoral in character. In contrast, his handling of the approach road shows a mastery of the picturesque. The road hugs the natural valleys in a gradual rise to the house of two hundred and fifty feet over a distance of three miles. By adding and improving upon pools and streams, and by planting to achieve a luxuriant, layered growth of vegetation, Olmsted enhanced the existing attributes of the site to create the impression of travelling through a deep, natural forest. A vast nursery was established to supply the demands of the landscaping operations at Biltmore. It was supervised by Chauncey Delos Beadle who became superintendent of the grounds at Biltmore from 1890, when work first started, until 1950. He was involved in the collection of numerous species of native plants, in particular of azaleas. In 1940 he gave his collection to the estate, and it is planted in the area that Olmsted called the 'Glen', beyond the shrub garden. It is largely thanks to the continuity of care that Beadle provided that the realisation of Olmsted's design for the Biltmore estate remains close to his original concept.

Restoration and maintenance

Today the farming operation at Biltmore concentrates more on crops and the re-establishment of a nursery than on livestock. There are three herds of beef cattle but the calving barn has been converted into a restaurant and the dairy into a winery. In 1987 a five year programme of restoration and maintenance was drawn up by the landscape department. It included the development of a master plan for the whole of the policies. The stated goals for the landscape restoration programme in 1989 were an increase in staff and staff training and preparation for the implementation of restoration projects, the continuation of research and site analysis, and an increase in nursery production for future planting. The estate has thus recognised the need to employ staff who are conversant with, and sympathetic to, conservation issues. Moreover it has been fortunate in being able to harness the studies of graduate, university landscape students to research projects at Biltmore. Ohio State University is carrying out a site survey and an assessment of the estate's development potential, aided by a grant from the Biltmore Company. The University of Tennessee has been approached to investigate the use of a computer program to record an up-to-date plan of the gardens. One student has taken the approach road as the subject of her Master's thesis and made recommendations for its treatment, and another is working on the indexing of all the archival material. Biltmore is well documented by photographs as well as by plans and correspondence. It is only in his intentions for the management of the planting that Olmsted's plans are incomplete.

Planting

Along the approach road Olmsted planted many climbers (*Lonicera japonica, Akebia quinata, Ampelopsis* and *Celastrus species*), no doubt designed to achieve a lush effect quickly, but in fact so vigorous as to become weeds. It may have been Olmsted's intention to take these out as other plants became established, but this was never done and the planting had become a jungle with vines choking many of the trees. The smaller shrubs too had become a dense undergrowth. Some of these have now been cleared so that massed planting gives way to grassy spaces, and the ponds and pools, many of which had silted up through lack of management, are being reclaimed, restoring the variety of the original scheme. As the road nears the edge of the forest the planting

74 The walled garden at Biltmore

75 New road signs shout their message

gradually thins out, and becomes scattered as the road reaches the boundaries of the farmland. Of the original species planted, not all were hardy, and a few have been lost. It is not intended to attempt to regrow these as the overall concept of the planting is considered more important than individual species, but new replacement plantings, particularly of trees, have been made, using the correct varieties where possible. Periods of drought cause the loss of many trees although the effect is often hidden for several years until the weakened specimens fall in a storm. In expanding the nursery the estate is anticipating the need to replant when the full impact of recent severe drought becomes evident.

The original planting design for the four acre walled garden followed the precedent of a typical English kitchen garden, and included fruit and vegetables. However, George Vanderbilt decided that he wanted an ornamental, rather than a productive, garden. The walled garden therefore became predominantly a flower garden soon after its inauguration. The garden is divided into quarters by vine arbours which were reconstructed on the original foundations in 1980 by the estate's carpentry staff. Many of the original grape vines survive and others have been propagated from them. In the late autumn 50,000 tulips are planted in the upper half of the garden. New bulbs are imported from Holland each year. Annuals for summer bedding are raised in the greenhouses and planted out in May. Two thousand roses of more than eighty varieties occupy the lower half of the garden. Part of this display are the roses which have won the All America Rose Society awards. There are perennial borders around the perimeter walks and *Pyracantha*, *Hypericum* and espaliered fruit trees along the walls. The latter require trimming six times a year. Care of the roses is intensive with daily deadheading to prolong the blooming period as well as watering, fertilisation and spraying. In the late 1960s and early 1970s climbers and ivy were stripped off the walls. Boston ivy is still a problem as it keeps growing back. It is planned to renew the herbaceous borders and gradually to increase the number of older varieties of annuals, perennials, roses and ornamental grasses and to add sod borders to make the garden more distinctively Victorian.

Irrigation systems are being installed as part of the current five year programme. An eight-foot-high deer fence is being constructed around all the garden areas to allow the replanting of the original herbaceous and ground cover plants in the shrub garden and other areas outwith the walled garden which have no other protection from browsing. The fence is well sited in the woodland so that it is not visually intrusive.

Visitors

Various means are used to publicise the estate. Regular press releases are issued to the media and promotional leaflets are available in all the local motels. A 'Victorian Christmas' is reproduced every year in December and in the spring there is a weekend festival of flowers. Visitors buy their entrance tickets at the gatehouse in Biltmore village and are then free to use their cars within the grounds. The estate signs have been redesigned to be read more easily by drivers, and the new metal ovals, maroon on white, are certainly less discreet than the old timber signs with yellow lettering. There are car parks at the gatehouse, gardens, restaurant and winery, but at present cars clutter the area in front of the house and spoil the sweeping prospect of the 'rampe douce'. The feasibility of a transit system is under consideration. A seven to ten acre single site would be necessary in a reasonable location for access which could also be suitably screened. The estate's greatest challenge lies in finding the balance between conservation and the running of a successful commercial operation. Staff are already conscious of an increasing litter problem as more visitors are attracted by new developments such as the winery. There were no historic precedents for the production of Biltmore wine, but it shows conservation at its most forward looking, where an extension of the farming enterprise and the imaginative re-use of existing buildings contribute to the vitality of the estate as a whole and ensure the resources for the more esoteric restoration measures.

FAIRSTED

Location, ownership and management

The Frederick Law Olmsted National Historic Site of 'Fairsted', which Olmsted made his office in 1883, is in Brookline, Massachusetts. The site is small, a two-acre suburban corner plot, which attracted Olmsted because of its picturesque character. He managed to persuade the owners to sell the property only by building them a new home on the south west boundary. Fairsted housed the premises of the Olmsted firm, through father, sons, and successive partners, until 1979 when the last partner was bought out and the National Park service acquired the site. The office buildings hold the records of five thousand projects in forty-seven states in the USA and Canada. The park rangers concentrate on the presentation of Olmsted as a landscape architect and co-operate with others, such as the rangers for the Boston Parks, on landscape interpretation. Groups are expected to make advance reservations for visits. Otherwise the site is open for three afternoons per week and entertains five thousand individual visitors a year. In addition staff receive three to five research requests daily due to increasing interest in the conservation of Olmsted's designs throughout the country.

Description and history

Olmsted was born in 1822 but it was not until 1865 that he was appointed landscape architect for Central Park, New York, his first commission, so he started his landscape career late. Although he was at Fairsted only twelve years before his retirement, this was during his most active and established period of work. Olmsted is best known for his park designs, but he was equally concerned with the improvement of the suburbs and the design of individual housing sites. Fairsted represents the principles he applied to these small scale designs. When Olmsted bought the property it was laid out as an orchard. He removed the fruit trees and planted shade trees along the boundaries. The new house, designed by John Charles Olmsted, was set on the crest of a steep slope and approached by a circular drive from the corner entrance. An open sweep of lawn embraced the property on the south. Below the house to the north was a 'hollow', planted with shade loving species, and on the eastern boundary was a densely planted rockery. Although the planting was altered and renewed over the years, and the test garden where the firm experimented with different plantings gave way to a parking lot, the layout remained essentially the same. After the 1930s the landscape was largely neglected for thirty years until, in the 1960s, substantial changes were made which altered the character of the site. The addition of flowering shrubs and perennials interrupted the flowing nature of the layered shrub borders and a swimming pool and terrace were built on the south lawn, with an annual and herb garden adjacent.

Restoration and maintenance

Planning

A 'General Management Plan' was prepared for the site in 1983, outlining a policy for the restoration of the buildings and grounds as they were in 1960 before major alteration. The year 1960 was chosen as it marked the end of the period when the Olmsted family were directly involved with the firm, but further research revealed serious drawbacks in adhering to this date. Very little documentation for the

76 Fairsted from the south lawn

77 The Hollow

landscape was produced after the late 1920s, and the deterioration of the landscape between then and 1960 meant that a restoration to 1960 would have been based on an unacceptable level of guesswork. It was therefore decided to revise the restoration date to 1930 when all the office buildings were complete, the landscape was well documented, and, despite modifications, still retained the basic character of Olmsted's design for the property.

A 'Grounds Maintenance Manual' was written by Rudi Favretti in 1986. It detailed maintenance techniques, a week by week annual programme of work, and specific plant lists and requirements. The rehabilitation of the house and grounds was just reaching a crucial stage when the change of policy on the restoration date was agreed in 1987. The house was about to be repainted and a decision had to be taken on the resurfacing of the car park which had turned to mud. The new policy saw the outside of the house painted a handsome dark red with a dark green trim, rather than the monotone grey-brown of the 1960s. The car park was finished with gravel as in 1930, but it was laid over a new substructure with drainage pipes. A metal edging strip has also been used where paths have been relaid in a concession to the higher standards of maintenance expected by the modern visitor.

Research documents

The spread of documentation available for the landscape is surprisingly uneven. Overall plans exist for 1883, 1887 and 1904. The 1904 plan shows the topography and massing of shrubs, but it was drawn up by surveyors who made several errors in plant identification. Copies of the 1904 plan were used to record new proposals or alterations up to the 1930s, but it is difficult to differentiate between actual conditions and new proposals. There are a considerable number of photographs from Olmsted senior's time, some from the 1920s and a few from the 1960s, but substantial areas of the site are not covered. From the photographs it is known that wisteria was grown on the house, and the devising of suitable supports so that it could be replaced without complicating the maintenance of the building posed problems. Spiral strapping wires support the vines on pipes fixed with a four-inch gap between them and the exterior clapboards.

Planting plans and computer mapping

Only a few of the original planting lists were cross-referenced to plans and not all of them even indicate for which areas they were written.

They had to be compared with plans and photographs before planting plans for the Rock garden, Hollow, South lawn, and Circular drive could be drawn up. These plans are being transferred to a computer mapping system linked to a database devised by Chi Ho Sham and Michael Papaik of Boston University for application to the conservation and maintenance of small parks, using Fairsted as a prototype. Two staff are being trained in the use of the system which allows the storage of a base map, individual plant histories, and maintenance information by species, and the printing of plant lists, all of which can be constantly updated. The software package is inexpensive, four hundred dollars, and operates on a Mackintosh computer.

HERCULES GARDEN, BLAIR CASTLE

Location, ownership and management

Blair Castle, Perthshire, is the home of His Grace, the Duke of Atholl. The surrounding policies cover over a thousand hectares which were designed, laid out and planted during the eighteenth and nineteenth centuries as a setting for the castle. The creation of the Hercules Garden was part of the improvements to the estate made by the second Duke between his succession in 1724 and his death in 1764. The policies, together with land at Dunkeld which also forms part of the estate, are managed by the Atholl Estates Office. A gardener is employed for the maintenance of the garden ground adjoining the castle but his remit does not extend to the Hercules Garden which remains in a derelict condition. Blair Castle is high on the list of Scotland's tourist attractions and entertains approximately 250,000 visitors a year, most of whom make a tour of the castle, but few of whom explore the fascinations of the various other features of the historic landscape.

Description and history

Although the boundaries of the Hercules Garden are walled, its size alone, roughly 3.65 hectares, immediately imbues it with a different character from that of the typical Scottish walled garden. This distinction is emphasised by the two ponds which occupy the central valley and, in the garden's heyday, was accentuated by the Chinese bridge on the main peninsula dividing them, the Chinese railing along the south wall, and the planting of the islands and peninsulas with trees such as laburnum and the weeping silver birch (*Betula pendula*), all of which recall the views depicted on Chinese laquerwork or porcelain. It is only from Hercules' vantage point of the central clairvoyée in the south wall that the walled, and approximately rectangular, form of the garden is obvious. From within, the ground slopes, the long canal pond curves, and the planting masks in such a way as to disguise the garden's length and to enhace its relationship to the surrounding hills despite the original, formal and very traditional, treatment of the walls and borders at both the west and east ends and the division of the garden into productive quarters by rows of fruit trees and bushes.

The statue of Hercules was erected by the second Duke in 1743, and work on the cutting of peats for the first pond began the following year. By 1748 the garden records clearly show the Duke's intention to move the walled garden away from the castle, and both the second, canal pond, and the first of the garden walls were under construction on the new site. By 1755 the garden was largely complete. The main features of the garden's original eighteenth-century layout, the walls, ponds, islands and peninsulas, are still extant and have undergone remarkably little change. In the late nineteenth century the north wall was rebuilt a few feet back from its original position and a terrace levelled by introducing a retaining wall in order to accommodate greenhouses. This alteration signalled a change of emphasis in the purpose of the garden from the enclosed 'ferme ornée', where the decorative element was an important and integral part, to productive walled garden, where the prime considerations were its use and maintenance. At the same time the building known as McGregor's Folly replaced the alcove in the east wall but, like the commemorative gates inserted in the south wall in 1924, these additions had little impact on the layout of the garden overall. The most devastating change on the layout was wrought in the 1950s when, after abandoning its post-war use as a market garden, a crop of Christmas trees was planted. The market collapsed and the trees were left unharvested until the Estate began to clear the garden in the 1980s.

The statue of Hercules and the garden walls, including the Gardener's House, Tool House and McGregor's Folly, are listed buildings. The Blair Castle landscape was included in the 'Preliminary and Interim List of Gardens and Parks of Outstanding Historic Interest' produced by ICOMOS in 1979, and subsequently recognised as 'outstanding' in the *Inventory of Gardens and Designed Landscapes in Scotland* prepared by Land Use Consultants in 1987. In 1989, with financial assistance from the Countryside Commission for Scotland, the Atholl Estates commissioned a report on the landscape with a view to formulating a management policy to promote the conservation of the historic design.

78   Aerial view of the Hercules Garden in 1946. © British Crown Copyright 1993

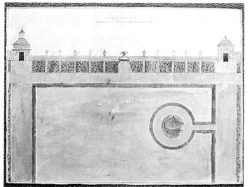

Drawings from the Castle archives:

79   The pond and wall at the west end of the garden. Watercolour plan c. 1748

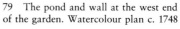

80   Detail of the design for the Chinese railing on the south wall, 1753

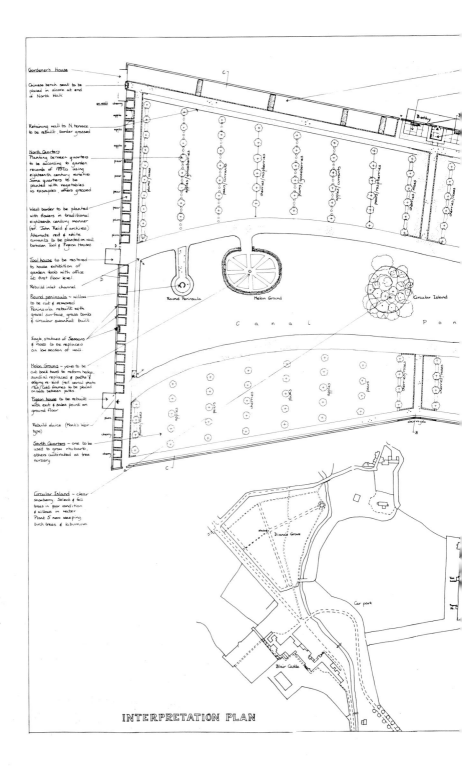

Gardener's House

Chinese bench seat to be placed in alcove at end of North Walk

Retaining wall to N. terrace to be rebuilt, border grassed

North Quarters
Planting between quarters to be according to garden records of 1950s using eighteenth century varieties. Some quarters to be planted with vegetables as examples, others grassed

West border to be planted with flowers in traditional eighteenth century manner (ref. John Reid & archives) Alternate red & white currants to be planted on wall between Tool & Pigeon Houses

Tool house to be restored to house exhibition of garden tools with office at first floor level

Rebuild inlet channel

Round peninsula – willow to be cut & removed. Peninsula rebuilt with gravel surface, grass banks & circular sundial built

Eagle, statues of Seasons & Vases to be replaced on low section of wall

Melon Ground – yews to be cut back hard to reform hedge, sundial replaced & paths & edging re-laid (ref aerial photo 1966) Cold frames to be placed on beds between paths

Pigeon house to be rebuilt with exit & sales point on ground floor

Rebuild sluice (Monk's Weir type)

South Quarters – one to be used to grow rhubarb, others cultivated as tree nursery

Circular Island – clear snowberry. Select & fell trees in poor condition & willows in water. Plant 5 new weeping birch trees & laburnum

Bothy

Round Peninsula   Melon Ground   Circular Island

C a n a l   P o n

plums/peaches   apples   cherries   plums   apples   pears   pears/strawberries   strawberries

plums/peaches   cherry   cherry

Diana's Grove

Car park

Blair Castle

INTERPRETATION PLAN

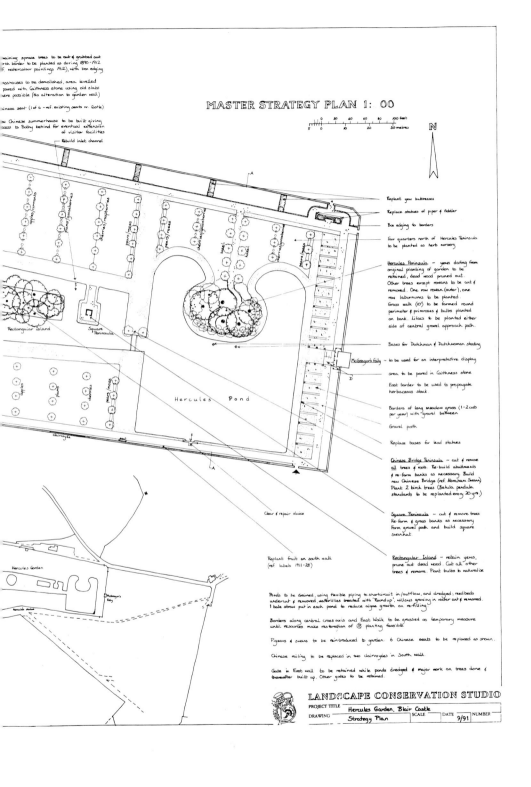

MASTER STRATEGY PLAN 1 : 00

0   20   40   60   80   100 feet
5   0   10   20   30 metres

N

...aining spruce trees to be cut & grubbed out
...rth border to be planted as during 1890-1912
... watercolour paintings 1912), with box edging

...asshouses to be demolished, area levelled
... paved with Caithness stone using old glass
...here possible (No alteration to garden wall)

...inese seat (1 of 6 - ref. existing seats nr. Castle)

... Chinese summerhouse to be built giving
...ccess to Bothy behind for eventual extension
... of visitor facilities

Rebuild inlet channel

Rectangular Island

Square Peninsula

Hercules   Pond

clairvoyee

Hercules Garden

McGregor's Folly

Hercules obelisk

Clear & repair sluice

Replant fruit on south wall
(ref. labels 1911-28)

Replant yew buttresses

Replace statues of piper & fiddler

Box edging to borders

Four quarters north of Hercules Peninsula
to be planted as herb nursery

Hercules Peninsula - yews dating from
original planting of garden to be
retained, dead wood pruned out.
Other trees except remains to be cut &
removed. One row rowan (outer), one
row laburnums to be planted.
Grass walk (10') to be formed round
perimeter & primroses & bulbs planted
on bank. Lilacs to be planted either
side of central gravel approach path.

Bases for Dutchman & Dutchwoman shading

McGregor's Folly - to be used for an interpretative display

area to be paved in Caithness stone

East border to be used to propagate
herbaceous stock.

Borders of long meadow grass (1-2 cuts
per year) with gravel between

Gravel path

Replace bases for lead statues

Chinese Bridge Peninsula - cut & remove
all trees & roots. Re-build abutments
& re-form banks as necessary. Build
new Chinese Bridge (ref. Abraham Swan).
Plant 2 birch trees (Betula pendula
standards to be replanted every 20 yrs)

Square Peninsula - cut & remove trees.
Re-form & grass banks as necessary.
Form gravel path and build square
summerhut.

Rectangular Island - retain yews,
prune out dead wood. Cut all other
trees & remove. Plant bulbs to naturalise

Ponds to be drained, using flexible piping to shortcircuit in/outflow, and dredged; reed beds
undercut & removed, waterlillies treated with 'Roundup', willows growing in water cut & removed.
1 bale straw put in each pond to reduce algae growth on re-filling

Borders along central cross axis and East Walk to be grassed as temporary measure
until resources make restoration of (8) planting feasible

Pigeons & swans to be reintroduced to garden. 6 Chinese seats to be replaced as shown.

Chinese railing to be replaced in two clairvoyees in South Wall.

Gate in East Wall to be retained while ponds dredged & major work on trees done &
thereafter built up. Other gates to be retained.

LANDSCAPE CONSERVATION STUDIO

PROJECT TITLE	Hercules Garden, Blair Castle				
DRAWING	Strategy Plan	SCALE		DATE 9/91	NUMBER

The report identified the conservation of the Hercules Garden as a major priority, and in 1990 consultants were appointed to develop a conservation strategy for the garden.

Restoration – research and planning

After considerable further research in the archives at Blair Castle and an extensive survey of the physical attributes of the site, the topography, buildings and vegetation, the following policy for the conservation of the garden was agreed between Atholl Estates and the consultants:

The conservation of the Hercules Garden is dependent for its success on the interest of visitors and its productive management. The restoration of the garden should embrace the extraordinary and exotic eighteenth-century vision of the garden's creation by returning it to a productive ferme ornée, embellished by both traditional and Chinese inspired features. Without detriment to the spirit of the original concept, the most significant features of the garden's subsequent history should be retained. Wherever possible the restoration of the garden should follow historical precedents, based firstly on a survey of the garden's surviving features, secondly on historical research of documents specific to the garden, and lastly on historical research of other relevant sources. Visitors should be encouraged to exercise imagination in understanding the eighteenth century origins of the garden, its later history and restoration, both through the approach and access to the garden and by its presentation. The planting should be restored and maintained to enhance these aims, balancing the constraints of cost and labour with the garden's potential for productivity.

The report, completed in 1992, proposes that advantage should be taken of the clear division between the main part of the garden and the north terrace, the eighteenth and nineteenth centuries, to present to the visitor the differences in character, especially in the planting of these two periods. From the clairvoyée at the Hercules statue it will be possible to differentiate between the two main periods of the garden's development while, since the line of the walk along the north terrace remains the same, the visitor will be able to comprehend the original eighteenth-century concept in the vistas across the garden to the south. It is proposed that the decorative element of the 'ferme ornée' should once again become of prime importance although the garden should be productive as far as possible. Later additions or alterations are therefore to be retained or removed on the basis of their contribution to, or detraction from, the eighteenth-century idea, but always with the aim of clearly presenting the development of the garden to the visitor. The main structural planting will be restored in phases, depending in part on the existing trees, with those from the eighteenth century conserved as long as is compatible with safety. The planting of the quarters and borders will seek to balance an adequate demonstration of the two periods of historical planting with considerations for simplifying maintenance, and the management plan will include provision for the eventual total replacement of planting when the mature trees on the islands and peninsulas are no longer viable, as well as for the modification of the treatment of certain areas of the garden in the light of archaeological investigations. The production of Hercules Garden preserves and plants for sale, and the leasing of some of the quarters as a tree nursery, under a strictly controlled agreement, are recommended as means of obtaining some financial income over and above entry fees from visitors.

It is hoped that a detailed management programme will be drawn up to initiate the report's recommendation for the first year in 1992. They include carrying out urgent work to the buildings and trees, the dredging of the ponds, the preparation of an archaeological brief, detailed design drawings and specifications, making applications for grant aid, deciding the means of implementation for the restoration and the appointment of a project manager. The project is an exciting one and the first of its kind in Scotland. Sponsorship for its conservation by the various funding bodies could pioneer the realistic recognition of the rich heritage of gardens in Scotland.

Conclusion

And work of the dead to pleasure the living,
A half-finished garden, epitaph, promise.
Brendan Kennelly

A garden is only ever half-finished, half-grown, half-decayed, unless it disappears, forgotten through heedless neglect. It is this quality of a half-complete picture which gives gardens their charm and their conservation its challenge. In the public eye the restoration of a garden is still too often thought synonymous with cleaning up. The riches of this facet of our cultural and artistic heritage are still too little recognised and understood. Gardens proliferate, but there are few examples of historic or aesthetically outstanding ones compared with the quantity of gardens in a modern idiom. The study and intelligent conservation of these few must be given priority if we respect our cultural roots.

In Scotland the number of gardens listed in the Inventory and lost since its publication in 1987 is alarming, particularly since the compilers of the Inventory themselves did not pretend to present more than a fraction of the gardens worthy of attention. How many important gardens perish unrecognised? It is imperative to create a climate of understanding and recognition of the significance of designed landscapes. Unfortunately the shrieking of one lobby can drown the feeble protestations of another if public and government awareness as to the value and true nature of the landscape is limited. Scottish Natural Heritage has yet to show its hand, but the proposals for the new agency, combining the roles of the Countryside Commission for Scotland and the Nature Conservancy Council, seemed in danger of ignoring the conservation of gardens altogether. Whether this is in part the result of the dominance of a richer neighbour with a romantic view of 'wild' Scottish landscape is irrelevant. The Scots will be guilty of connivance in the demise of a

82   The decorative, re-created vegetable garden at Mount Vernon

rich part of their heritage if they do not protest, not just the managed nature but the deliberate, aesthetic design of much of their country-side.

If ignorance is parlous, so too is inaction. The Italians are at risk of strangling practical garden conservation at birth by insisting on tying it to an agreed theory. Whereas much can be destroyed by hasty moves to 'restore' as was the case with many of the garden re-creations of the 1930s, even more may be put in jeopardy if nothing is done at all. This danger has been the reason for an increasing advocation of a 'conserve as found' policy. As in other fields of knowledge, the principles of conservation develop through trial and error, and the process of con-servation itself has much to teach of the history of garden design and garden making. Nevertheless, differences of attitude to conservation are invaluable. We have the Italians to thank for the most comprehensive written survey of garden conservation issues. The Americans have much to teach in their harnessing of a national interest in historic personalities to the cause of garden conservation, and the Germans are setting an example of how to walk a conservation tightrope with a vociferous environmental lobby.

The enormous variety of gardens is reflected in the variety of approaches to their conservation. Much is to be gained by examining the results of different types of intervention since, with increasing knowledge and the development of new methods in archaeology, construction and chemical control, the conservation of gardens is both facilitated and complicated. Although modern technology has its place, often, as in the reconstruction of the surface of the grotto at Painshill, original techniques are the most efficacious. On the other hand, the use of modern insecticides, for example, has helped to preserve rare plant species and to maintain the diversity of the available genetic pool.

The conservation of gardens is now sufficiently established to have its own history which can profitably be explained to a wider public. At Mount Vernon there is a promising intention to present the vegetable garden, with its strong decorative element, as a re-creation typical of the colonial revivalist movement of the 1930s. Where this type of presentation has been tried elsewhere it has been notably successful in increasing interest, and it is to be hoped that the perpetration of misinformation – the illusion that Pitmedden, for example, represents a seventeenth-century garden – should cease. Above all, clarity is the most important quality in the conservation of heritage gardens: clarity in the assessment of the problem and the weighing of the pros and cons in the choice of a conservation policy; clarity in the setting of design objectives; clarity of execution, and clarity of presentation. For clarity throughout the conservation process can best ensure that the epitaph of our gardens is not further eroded, and the promise of their continuing contribution to our cultural heritage is realised.

Notes

1 Background

1 The correct French term is 'jardin à l'anglaise', but 'jardin anglais' rapidly came into common usage elsewhere.
2 William Blake, 'Jerusalem'.
3 Gilpin's accounts of his tours were not published until the 1790s although he made his tours earlier.
4 E. Kemp, *Gardener's Chronicle* 1857–62.
5 Janette Gallagher, 'Visiting Historic Gardens', Research Paper, Leeds Polytechnic, 1983.
6 American terminology for 'conservation' as defined in the glossary.
7 Now 'Historic Scotland'.
8 Highclere Park, Hampshire.
9 See Selected sources of further information, pp. 169–70.
10 Blenheim Study, Cobham Resource Consultants and Colvin and Moggridge.
11 See *Directory of Grant Making Trusts*, Charities Aid Foundation. Address on p. 169.
12 Amalgamated with the Nature Conservancy Council for Scotland to form 'Scottish Natural Heritage' in April 1992.
13 Quaderni 3, *Giardini Italiani*, Ministero per i Beni Culturali e Ambientali, 1981.

2 The conservation process

1 These can be obtained from Aerofilms Ltd, Gate Studio, Station Road, Boreham, Herts WD6 1ET and the Air Photographs Unit of the Scottish Development Department.

3 Maintenance and management

1 Weed Research Organisation, Oxford.
2 See page 113.
3 Arboricultural research note 40/81/ARB – DOE Arboricultural Advisory and Information Service.
4 Arboricultural research note 59/85/ARB.

4 Case studies

1 See page 74.
2 See page 43.

Selected sources of further information

United Kingdom

Publications

Bibliography of British Gardens, Ray Desmond 1984.

Directory of Grant Making Trusts, Charities Aid Foundation, 48 Pembury Road, Tonbridge, Kent TN9 2JD.

Directory of Social Change, 9 Mansfield Place, London NW3.

Landscape Specification, Landscape Promotions, Stirling University Innovation Park, Scottish Metropolitan Beta Centre, Innovation Park, Stirling FK9 4NF.

Researching a Garden's History Through Documentary and Published Sources, Landscape Design Trust, 5a West Street, Reigate, Surrey RH2 9BL.

The Plant Finder, Hardy Plant Society, c/o Lakeside, Gaines Road, Whitbourne, Worcestershire WR6 5RD.

Organisations

Arboricultural Advisory and Information Service, Forestry Commission, Forest Research Station, Alice Holt Lodge, Wrecclesham, Farnham, Surey GU10 4LH.

Centre for the Conservation of Historic Parks and Gardens, Institute of Advanced Architectural Studies, University of York, The King's Manor, York YO1 2EP.

Centre for Environmental Interpretation, Manchester Polytechnic, Bellhouse Building, Lower Ormond Street, Manchester M15 6BX.

Countryside Commission, John Dower House, Crescent Place, Cheltenham, Gloucestershire GL50 3RA.

English Heritage, Fortress House, 23 Savile Row, London W1X 2HE.

Garden History Society, 5 The Knoll, Hereford HR1 1RU.

The Hampshire Gardens Trust, 3rd Floor, Technology House, Victoria Road, Winchester SO23 7DU.

Historic Houses Association, 38 Ebury Street, London SW1 0LU.

Historic Scotland, 20 Brandon Street, Edinburgh EH3 5RA.

National Council for the Conservation of Plants and Gardens, RHS Garden, Wisley, Nr Woking, Surrey GU23 6QB.

National Monuments Record for Wales, Royal Commission on Ancient and Historical Monuments in Wales, Edelston House, Queens Road, Aberystwyth, Dyfed SY23 2HP.

National Monuments Record of Scotland, Royal Commission on the Ancient and Historical Monuments of Scotland, John Sinclair House, 16 Bernard Terrace, Edinburgh EH8 9NX.

National Trust Estates Advisers Office, Spitalgate Lane, Cirencester GL7 2DE.

Scottish Natural Heritage (formerly

Countryside Commission for Scotland),
Battleby, Redgorton, Perth PH1 3EW.

The Welsh Historical Gardens Trust, Rose
Cottage, Blancyfelin, Carmarthen, Dyfed
SA33 5ND.

United States of America

Publications

Cultural Resource Bibliography, Park Historic
Architecture Division, US Department of the
Interior, National Park Service, PO Box 37127,
Washington DC 20013–7127.

Friends of Historic Landscapes Directory, as
above.

Organisations

National Register of Historic Places, US
Department of the Interior, National Park
Service, PO Box 37127, Washington DC
20013–7127.

National Trust for Historic Preservation,
Office of Development and Communications,
1785, Massachusetts Avenue NW, Washington
DC 20036.

*The Thomas Jefferson Center for Historic
Plants,* Monticello, PO Box 316,
Charlottesville, VA 22902.

Seed Savers Exchange, PO Box 70, Decorah,
IA 52101.

Eire

Irish Architectural Archive, 75 Merrion
Square, Dublin 2.

Germany

*Institut für Grünplanung und
Gartenarchitektur,* Universität Hannover,
Herrenhäuser Strasse 2A, 3000 Hannover 21.

Further reading

The History of Gardens, Christopher Thacker 1979 – general, readable and a good introduction

The Italian Renaissance Garden, Claudia Lazzaro 1990 – sumptuous <u>and</u> scholarly

Italian Gardens, Georgina Masson 1961 – the pioneering work, now a classic

Princely Gardens: The Origins and Development of the French Formal Style, Kenneth Woodbridge 1986 – outstanding, a comprehensive study

The Gardens of William and Mary, David Jacques and Ahrend J. van der Horst 1988 – a well illustrated account by several authors which sets the gardens in their historical context and goes right down to planting detail

Georgian Gardens: The Reign of Nature, David Jaques 1983 – a thorough work, well researched

Georgian Gardens, David Stuart 1979 – an enjoyable read covering most aspects including planting

British and American Gardens in the Eighteenth Century, edited by Robert P. Maccubbin and Peter Martin 1984 – an excellent collection of essays, subjects include garden history as a discipline and landscape archaeology

The Landscape Garden in Scotland 1735–1835, A. A. Tait 1980 – an academic approach but one of the very few books on Scottish gardens

Victorian Gardens, Brent Elliot 1986 – deservedly recognised as an authority

The Garden Triumphant: A Victorian Legacy, David Stuart 1988 – an amusing read, gives the flavour of the period

Tutela dei Giardini Storici: Bilanci e Prospettive, edited by Vincenzo Cazzato 1989 Ministero per i Beni Culturali e Ambientali, Ufficio Studi – a collection of short essays, essential reading for the history and theory of conservation

Gartendenkmalpflege: Grundlagen der Erhaltung historischer Gärten und Grünanlagen, edited by Dieter Hennebo 1985 – heavy going in parts, especially if your knowledge of German is less than perfect, but both theory and practice covered, worth having for the illustrations alone

Landscapes and Gardens for Historic Buildings, Rudy J. and Joy P. Favretti 1978 – a good basic text, a little bit of everything

Large Gardens and Parks: Maintenance, Management and Design, Tom Wright 1981 – <u>the</u> practical handbook on management and maintenance, due for an up-date

Plants from the Past, David Stuart and James Sutherland 1987 – a selective descriptive list

National Register Bulletin 18: 'How to Evaluate and Nominate Designed Historic Landscapes', US Dept. of Interior, National Park Service – a useful starting point for assessment

The following journals and magazines contain useful articles on garden history or conservation topics:

Further reading

The Journal of Garden History

Garden History – the journal of the Garden History Society

The Garden – the journal of the Royal Horticultural Society

Country Life

Landscape Research

Historic Preservation – journal of the National Trust for Historic Preservation

Index

Index

Index

research, documentary 72–3; case studies 120, 126–8, 132–4, 139, 144, 156, 162; maintenance 82; organisations 44–6; planting 67–8, 73
restoration 2, 38, 44, 46, 55–6, 58, 60; case studies 110–14, 115–18, 120–2, 126–8, 130–5, 139–42, 144–7, 150–3, 154–7, 162–3
'restoration-in-spirit' 58
Robins, Thomas 29
Robinson, William 36
Rococo 29, 104
Rosa, Salvator 25, 26, 130
rose 70, 82, 110–12, 152
rosemary 10
Rousham 25
Royal Botanical Society of Manchester and the Northern Counties 138
Royal Horticultural Society 44
Rozendaal 29
ruins (picturesque) 26, 30, 124, 125, 133, 134

Sackville-West, Vita 98, 120
Saint-Germain-en-Laye 14
sandstone 71, 114
Schleissheim, Munich 17, 116
Schloss Augustusberg, Brühl 17, 115–18
Schloss Dyck 34
Schloss Linderhof 84
Schlossgarten Schwetzingen 2, 66, 103–8, 109
Scotland 2, 4, 18–24, 28–9, 30, 36, 43, 44, 45, 47, 48, 49, 52, 63–6, 68, 86, 164–5; case study 157–63
Scott, Sir Walter 32
Scottish Development Department 45, 47
Scottish Natural Heritage 164, 169
Scottish Tourist Board 47
sculpture 3, 13, 29, 31, 38, 100, 113–14
Seed Savers Exchange 70
Sequoia 140
Serlio, Sebastiano 10
serpentine paths and walks 22, 24, 30
Seton, Sir Alexander 20, 66
Shenstone, William 26
Sibbald Robert 68
Sissinghurst 98, 120
Sitwell, George 36
Sitwell, Sir Osbert 36
Society for the Interpretation of

Britain's Heritage 46
sod borders 152
Sophie, Electress of Hanover 17, 110
Spain 8
staff (labour) 83–4, 101–2
Stichting Particuliere Historische Buitenplaatsen 46
Stourhead 25–6, 56, 68
Stowe 25
Studley Royal 26, 88, 97
survey, aerial photography 74; archaeological 74–5; field 44, 55, 72, 74, 162; plans and records 72–3, 75–6; preliminary 45, 53–4; vegetation 74, 95
sweet chestnut 16
Switzer, Stephen 22, 24
sycamore (*Acer*) 124

Tatton Garden Society 138
Taymouth 25
theft 100
Thomas Jefferson Centre for Historic Plants 41, 142, 147–8
Thomas Jefferson Memorial Foundation 41, 142, 144
Tivoli (Villa d'Este) 8, 9
tools (cultivation) 83, 86
topiary 18, 22, 34, 90, 91
Tree Preservation Orders 49, 140
trees 28, 104–6, 128, 130, 150–2, 154, 157–8; avenues 56, 114; cultivation 24, 86; establishment 94; exotics 17, 25, 28; fruit 66–7, 143, 146, 158; loss and damage 88–9, 92, 98; planting 92, 146; protection 93–4; pruning 95–6; retention and replacement 56, 77, 91, 93; survey 74, 134; transplanting 94
Trequanda 4
Trianon 16
Triggs, Inigo 34
Trustees of Public Reservations 43
Tuileries 14
tulips 17, 64, 152
tulip tree 146

Utens, Giusto 8, 10, 20

Vanbrugh 25, 28
vandalism 94, 99, 101
Vanderbilt, George 148, 152
Vaux-le-Vicomte 14, 38, 40, 53
vegetables 36, 147
Versailles 12, 14–16, 41

video tapes 62, 135
Vieilles Maisons Françaises 47
Vignola 8
Villa Capponi, Arcetri 6, 7
Villa Castello 8, 10
Villa d'Este, Tivoli 8, 9
Villa Gamberaia, Settignano 6
Villa La Petraia 20, 91, 93
Villa Lante, Bagnaia 8, 9
Villa Ruspoli 8–10
Villandry 12, 38, 39
vines and vineyards 135, 146, 147, 152
Virgil 22, 26
visitors 26, 28, 40–3, 56, 63, 76, 83, 84, 91, 100, 101–2; case studies 103, 108, 119, 120, 121, 122, 124, 135, 139–40, 142–3, 148, 153, 154, 157, 162; wear and tear 56, 89, 90, 92; *see also* presentation
von Sckell, Friedrich Ludwig 17, 104, 106

Wales 43, 45, 47
wallflowers 66, 112
Wardian case 32
Washington, George 30, 41, 68
water features 6, 8, 9, 10, 16, 18, 28, 97, 106, 110, 113, 115–17, 132, 149, 150, 157–9
weed control 84–7, 113
weeding 84, 86
Weikersheim 29, 31
Weldam, Holland 34
Welsh Development Agency 46
West Germany 2, 17, 29, 42, 45, 48, 49–50, 66, 86; case studies 103–18
Westbury Court 18, 53
Whately, Thomas 143
wilderness 22, 24, 30
wild hyacinth 74
William and Mary 18
Williamsburg 39, 40, 143
Wisley 44
wisteria 156
Woodland Grant Scheme 47
Wright, Tom 82
wrought iron 10
wych elm (*Ulmus glabra*) 98

Yester House 20, 21
yew (*Taxus*) 16, 18, 90, 91, 98, 116, 130, 140
Youth Training Scheme (YTS) 46, 136
yucca 147

Zeyher, Johann Michael 104, 105, 106

176